Internationa

Hartley Withers

Alpha Editions

This edition published in 2022

ISBN : 9789356576087

Design and Setting By
Alpha Editions
www.alphaedis.com
Email – info@alphaedis.com

PREFACE

Responsibility for the appearance of this book—but not for its contents—lies with the Council for the Study of International Relations, which asked me to write one "explaining what the City really does, why it is the centre of the world's Money Market," etc. In trying to do so, I had to go over a good deal of ground that I had covered in earlier efforts to throw light on the machinery of money and the Stock Exchange; and the task was done amid many distractions, for which readers must make as kindly allowance as they can.

HARTLEY WITHERS.

6, LINDEN GARDENS, W.
March, 1916.

CHAPTER I

CAPITAL AND ITS REWARD

Finance, in the sense in which it will be used in this book, means the machinery of money dealing. That is, the machinery by which money which you and I save is put together and lent out to people who want to borrow it. Finance becomes international when our money is lent to borrowers in other countries, or when people in England, who want to start an enterprise, get some or all of the money that they need, in order to do so, from lenders oversea. The biggest borrowers of money, in most countries, are the Governments, and so international finance is largely concerned with lending by the citizens of one country to the Governments of others, for the purpose of developing their wealth, building railways and harbours or otherwise increasing their power to produce.

Money thus saved and lent is capital. So finance is the machinery that handles capital, collects it from those who save it and lends it to those who want to use it and will pay a price for the loan of it. This price is called the rate of interest, or profit. The borrower offers this price because he hopes to be able, after paying it, to benefit himself out of what he is going to make or grow or get with its help, or if it is a Government because it hopes to improve the country's wealth by its use. Sometimes borrowers want money because they have been spending more than they have been getting, and try to tide over a difficulty by paying one set of creditors with the help of another, instead of cutting down their spending. This path, if followed far enough, leads to bankruptcy for the borrower and loss to the lender.

If no price were offered for capital, we should none of us save, or if we saved we should not risk our money by lending it, but hide it in a hole, or lock it up in a strong room, and so there could be no new industry.

Since capital thus seems to be the subject-matter of finance and it is the object of this book to make plain what finance does, and how, it will be better to begin with clear understanding of the function of capital. All the more because capital is nowadays the object of a good deal of abuse, which it only deserves when it is misused. When it is misused, let us abuse it as heartily as we like, and take any possible measures to punish it. But let us recognize that capital, when well and fairly used, is far from being a sinister and suspicious weapon in the hands of those who have somehow managed to seize it; but is in fact so necessary to all kinds of industry, that those who have amassed it, and placed it at the disposal of industry render a service to society without which society could not be kept alive.

For capital, as has been said, is money saved and lent to, or employed in, industry. By being lent to, or employed in, industry it earns its rate of interest or profit. There are nowadays many wise and earnest people who think that this interest or profit taken by capital is not earned at all but is wrung out of the workers by a process of extortion. If this view is correct then all finance, international and other, is organized robbery, and instead of writing and reading books about it, we ought to be putting financiers into prison and making a bonfire of their bonds and shares and stock certificates. But, with all deference to those who hold this view, it is based on a complete misapprehension of the nature and origin of capital.

Capital has been described above as money put to certain purposes. This was done for the sake of clearness and because this definition fits in with the facts as they usually happen in these days. Economists define capital as wealth reserved for production, and we must always remember that money is only a claim for, or a right to, a certain amount of goods or a certain amount of other people's work. Money is only a title to wealth, because if I have a sovereign or a one-pound note in my pocket, I thereby have the power of buying a pound's worth of goods or of hiring a doctor to cure me or a parson to bury me or anybody else to do anything that I want, up to the buying power of that sovereign. This is the power that money carries with it. When the owner of this power, instead of exercising it in providing himself with luxuries or amusements, uses it by lending it to someone who wants to build a factory, and employ workers, then, because the owner of the money receives his rate of interest he is said to be exploiting labour, because, so it is alleged, the workers work and he, the capitalist, sits in idleness and lives on their labour.

And so, in fact, he does. But we have not yet found out how he got the money that he lent. That money can only have been got by work done or services rendered, for which other people were ready to pay. Capital, looked at from this point of view, is simply stored up work, and entitled to its reward just as much as the work done yesterday. The capitalist lives on the work of others, but he can only do so because he has wrought himself in days gone by or because someone else has wrought and handed on to him the fruits of his labour. Let us take the case of a shopkeeper who has saved a hundred pounds. This is his pay for work done and risk taken (that the goods which he buys may not appeal to his customers) during the years in which he has saved it. He might spend his hundred pounds on a motor cycle and a side-car, or on furniture, or a piano, and nobody would deny his right to do so. On the contrary he would probably be applauded for giving employment to makers of the articles that he bought. Instead of thus consuming the fruit of his work on his own amusement, and the embellishment of his home, he prefers to make provision for his old age. He invests his hundred pounds in the 5 per cent. debenture stock of a company being formed to extend a boot factory. Thereby he gives employment to the people who build the extension and provide the machinery, and thereafter to the men and women who work in the factory, and moreover he is helping to supply other people with boots. He sets people to work to supply other people's wants instead of his own, and he receives as the price, of his service five pounds a year. But it is his work, that he did in the years in which he was saving, that is earning him this reward.

An interesting book has lately appeared in America, called "Income," in which the writer, Dr. Scott Nearing, of the University of Pennsylvania, draws a very sharp distinction between service income and property income, implying, if I read him aright, that property income is an unjust extortion. This is how he states his case:—[1]

> "The individual whose effort creates values for which society pays receives service income. His reward is a reward for his personality, his time, his strength. Railroad president and roadmender devote themselves to activities which satisfy the wants of their fellows. Their service is direct. In return for their hours of time and their calories of energy, they receive a share of the product which they have helped to produce.

> "The individual who receives a return because of his property ownership, receives a property income. This man has a title deed to a piece of unimproved land lying in the centre of a newly developing town. A storekeeper offers him a thousand dollars a year for the privilege of placing a store on the land. The owner of the land need make no exertion. He simply holds his title. Here a man has labored for twenty years and saved ten thousand dollars by denying himself the necessaries of life. He invests the money in railroad bonds, and someone insists he thereby serves society. In one sense he does serve. In another, and a larger sense, he expects the products of his past service (the twenty years of labor), to yield him an income. From the day when he makes his investment he need never lift a finger to serve his fellows. Because he has the investment, he has income. The same would hold true if the ten thousand dollars had been left him by his father or given to him by his uncle.... The fact of possession is sufficient to yield him an income."

Now, in all these cases of property income which Dr. Nearing seems to regard as examples of income received in return for no effort, there must have been an effort once, on the part of somebody, which put the maker of it in possession of the property which now yields an income to himself, or those to whom he has left or given it. First there is the case of the man who has a title deed to a piece of land. How did he get it? Either he was a pioneer who came and cleared it and settled on it, or he had worked and saved and with the product of his work had bought this piece of land, or he had inherited it from the man who had cleared or bought the land. The ownership of the land implies work and saving and so is entitled to its reward. Then there is the case of the man who has saved ten thousand dollars by labouring for twenty years and denying himself the necessaries of life. Dr. Nearing admits that this man has worked in order to get his dollars; he even goes so far as to add that he had denied himself the necessaries of life in order to save. Incidentally one may wonder how a man who has denied himself the necessaries of life for twenty years can be alive at the end of them. This man has worked for his dollars, and, instead of spending them on immediate enjoyment, lends them to people who are building a railway, and so is quickening and cheapening intercourse and trade. Dr. Nearing seems to admit grudgingly that in a sense he thereby renders a service, but he complains because his imaginary investor expects without further exertion to get an income from the product of his past service. If he could not get an income from it, why should he save? And if he and millions of others did not save how could railways or factories be built? And if there were no railways or factories how could workers find employment?

If every capitalist only got income from the product of his own work in the past, which he had spent, as in this case, on developing industry, his claim to a return on it would hardly need stating. He would have saved his ten thousand dollars or two thousand pounds, and instead of spending it on two thousand pounds' worth of amusement or pleasure for himself he would have preferred to put it at the disposal of those who are in need of capital for industry and promise to pay him 5 per cent. or £100 a year for the use of it. By so doing he increases the demand for labour, not momentarily as he would have done if he had spent his money on goods and services immediately consumed, but for all time, as long as the railway that he helps to build is running and earning an income by rendering services. He is a benefactor to humanity as long as his capital is invested in a really useful enterprise, and especially to the workers who cannot get work unless the organizers of industry are supplied with plenty of cheap capital. In fact, the more plentiful and cheap is capital, the keener will be the demand for the labour of the workers.

But when Dr. Nearing points out that the income of the ten thousand dollars would be equally secure if the owner of them had them left him by his father or given him by his uncle, then at last he smites capital on a weak point in its armour. There, is, without question, much to be said for the view that it is unfair that a man who has worked and saved should thereby be able to hand over to his son or nephew, who has never worked or saved, this right to an income which is derived from work done by somebody else. It seems unfair to all of us, who were not blessed with equally industrious and provident fathers and uncles, and it is often bad for the man who gets the income as a reward for no effort of his own, because it gives him a false start in life and sometimes tends to make him a futile waster, who can only justify his existence and his command over other people's work, by pointing to the efforts of his deceased sire or uncle. Further, unless he is very lucky, he is likely to grow up with the notion that, just because he has been left or given a certain income, he is somehow a superior person, and that it is part of the scheme of the universe that others should work for his benefit, and that any attempt on the part of other people to get a larger share, at his expense, of the good things of the earth is an attempt at robbery. He is, by being born to a competence, out of touch with the law of nature, which says that all living things must work for their living, or die, and his whole point of view is likely to be warped and narrowed by his unfortunate good fortune.

These evils that spring from hereditary property are obvious. But it may be questioned whether they outweigh the advantages that arise from it. The desire to possess is a strong stimulus to activity in production, because possession is the mark of success in it, and all healthy-minded men like to feel that they have succeeded; and almost equally strong is the desire to hand on to children or heirs the possessions that the worker's energy has got for him. In fact it may almost be said that in most men's minds the motive of possession implies that of being able to hand on; they would not feel that they owned property which they were bound to surrender to the State at their deaths. If and when society is ever so organized that it can produce what it needs without spurring the citizen to work with the inducement supplied by possession, and the power to hand on property, then it may be possible to abolish the inequities that hereditary property carries with it. As things are at present arranged it seems that we are bound to put up with them if the community is to be fed and kept alive. At least we can console ourselves with the thought that property does not come into existence by magic. Except in the case of the owners of land who may be enriched without any effort by the discovery of minerals or by the growth of a city, capital can only have been created by services rendered; and even in the case of owners of land, they, and those from whom they derived it, must have done something in order to get the land.

It is, of course, quite possible that the something which was done was a service which would not now be looked on as meriting reward. In the medieval days mailclad robbers used to get (quite honestly and rightly according to the notions then current) large grants of land because they had ridden by the side of their feudal chiefs when they went on marauding forays. In later times, as in the days of our Merry Monarch, attractive ladies were able to found ducal families by placing their charms at the service of a royal debauchee. But the rewards of the freebooters have in almost all cases long ago passed into the hands of those who purchased them with the proceeds of effort with some approach to economic justification; and though some of Charles the Second's dukedoms are still extant, it will hardly be contended that it is possible to trace the origin of everybody's property and confiscate any that cannot show a reasonable title, granted for some true economic service.

What we can do, and ought to do, if economic progress is to move along right lines, is to try to make sure that we are not, in these days of alleged enlightenment, committing out of mere stupidity and thoughtlessness, the crime which Charles the Second perpetrated for his own amusement. He gave large tracts of England to his mistresses because they pleased his roving fancy. Now the power to dispense wealth has passed into the hands of the people, who buy the goods and services produced, and so decide what goods and services will find a market, and so will enrich their producers. Are we making much better use of it? On the whole, much better; but we still make far too many mistakes. The people to whom nowadays we give big fortunes, though they include a large number of organizers of useful industry, also number within their ranks a crowd of hangers on such as bookmakers, sharepushers, and vendors of patent pills or bad stuff to read. These folk, and others, live on our vices and stupidities, and it is our fault that they can do so. Because a large section of the public likes to gamble away its money on the Stock Exchange, substantial fortunes have been founded by those who have provided the public with this means of amusement. Because the public likes to be persuaded by the clamour of cheapjack advertisement that its inside wants certain medicines, and that these medicines are worth buying at a price that makes the vendor a millionaire, there he is with his million. Some people say that he has swindled the public. The public has swindled itself by allowing him to foist stuff down its throat on terms which give him, and his heirs and assigns after him, all the control over the work and wealth of the world that is implied by the possession of a million. When we buy rubbish we do not only waste our money to our own harm, but, under the conditions of modern society, we put the sellers of rubbish in command of the world, as far as the money power commands it, which is a good deal further than is pleasing.

Hence it is that when some of those who question the right of capital to its reward, do so on the ground that capital is often acquired by questionable means, they are barking up the wrong tree. Capital can only be acquired by selling something to you and me. If you and I had more sense in the matter of what we buy, capital could not be acquired by questionable means. By our greed and wastefulness we give fortunes to bookmakers, market-riggers and money-lenders. By our preference for "brilliant" investments, with a high rate of interest and bad security, we invite the floating of rotten companies and waterlogged loans. By our readiness to be deafened by the clamour of the advertiser into buying things that we do not want, we hand industry over to the hands of the loudest shouter, and by our half-educated laziness in our selection of what we read and of the entertainments that we frequent, we open the way to opulence through the debauching of our taste and opinions. It is our fault and ours only. As soon as we have learnt and resolved to buy and enjoy only what is worth having, the sellers of rubbish may put up their shutters and burn their wares.

Capital, then, is stored up work, work that has been paid for by society. Those who did the work and took its reward, turned the proceeds of it into making something more instead of into pleasure and gratification for themselves. By a striking metaphor capital is often described as the seed corn of industry. Seed corn is the grain that the farmer, instead of making it into bread for his own table, or selling it to turn it into picture-palace tickets, or beer, or other forms of short-lived comfort, keeps to sow in the earth so that he may reap his harvest next year. If the whole world's crop were eaten, there would be no seed corn and no harvest. So it is with industry. If its whole product were turned into goods for immediate consumption, there could be no further development of industry, and no maintenance of its existing plant, which would soon wear out and perish. The man who spends less than he earns and puts his margin into industry, keeps industry alive.

From the point of view of the worker—by whom I mean the man who has little or no capital of his own, and has only, or chiefly, his skill, of head or of hand, to earn his living with—those who are prepared to save and put capital at the disposal of industry ought to be given every possible encouragement to do so. For since capital is essential to industry, all those who want to earn a living in the workshops or in the countinghouse, or in the manager's office, will most of all, if they are well advised, want to see as much capital saved as possible. The more there is of it, the more demand there will be for the brains and muscles of the workers, and the better the bargain these latter will be able to make for the use of their brains and muscles. If capital is so scarce and timid that it can only be tempted by the offer of high rates for its use, organizers of industry will think twice about expanding works or opening new ones, and there will be a check to the demand for workers. If so many people are saving that capital is a drug in the market, anyone who has an enterprise in his head will put it in hand, and workers will be wanted, first for construction then for operation.

It is to the interest of workers that there should be as many capitalists as possible offering as much capital as possible to industry, so that industry shall be in a state of chronic glut of capital and scarcity of workers. Roughly, it is true that the product of industry is divided between the workers who carry it on, and the savers who, out of the product of past work, have built the workshop, put in the plant and advanced the money to pay the workers until the new product is marketed. The workers and the savers are at once partners and rivals. They are partners because one cannot do without the other; rivals because they compete continually concerning their share of the profit realized. If the workers are to succeed in this competition and secure for themselves an ever-increasing share of the profit of industry—and from the point of view of humanity, civilization, nationality, and common sense it is most desirable that this should be so—then this is most likely to happen if the savers are so numerous that they will be weak in bargaining and unable to stand out against the demands of the workers. If there were innumerable millions of workers and only one saver with money enough to start one factory, the one saver would be able to name his own terms in arranging his wages bill, and the salaries of his managers and clerks. If the wind were on the other cheek, and a crowd of capitalists with countless millions of money were eager to set the wheels of industry going, and could not find enough workers to man and organize and manage their workshops, then the workers would have the whip hand. To bring this state of things about it would seem to be good policy not to damn the capitalist with bell and with book and frighten him till he is so scarce that he is master of the situation, but to give him every encouragement to save his money and put it into industry. For the more plentiful he is, the stronger is the position of the workers.

In fact the saver is so essential that it is nowadays fashionable to contend that the saving business ought not to be left to the whims of private individuals, but should be carried out by the State in the public interest; and there are some innocent folk who imagine that, if this were done, the fee that is now paid to the saver for the use of the capital that he has saved, would somehow or other be avoided. In fact the Government would have to tax the community to produce the capital required. Capital would be still, as before, the proceeds of work done. And the result would be that the taxpayers as a whole would have to pay for capital by providing it. This might be a more equitable arrangement, but as capital can only be produced by work, the taxpayers would have to do a certain amount of work with the prospect of not being allowed to keep the proceeds, but of being forced to hand it over to Government. Whether such a plan would be likely to be effective in keeping industry supplied with capital is a question which need not be debated until the possibility of such a system becomes a matter of practical politics.

For our present purpose it is enough to have shown that the capital, which is the stock-in-trade of finance, is not a fraudulent claim to take toll of the product of industry, but an essential part of the foundation on which industry is built. A man can only become a capitalist by rendering services for which he receives payment, and spending part of his pay not on his immediate enjoyment, but in establishing industry either on his own account or through the agency of someone else to whom be lends the necessary capital. Before any industry can start there must be tools and a fund out of which the workers can be paid until the work that they do begins to bring in its returns. The fund to buy these tools and pay the workers can only be found out of the proceeds of work done or services rendered. Moreover, there is always a risk to be run. As soon as the primitive savage left off making everything for himself and took to doing some special work, such as arrow making, in the hope that his skill, got from concentration on one particular employment, would be rewarded by the rest of the tribe who took his arrows and gave him food and clothes in return, he began to run the risk that his customers might not want his product, if they happened to take to fishing for their food instead of shooting it. This risk is still present with the organizers of industry and it falls first on the capitalist. If an industry fails the workers cease to be employed by it; but as long as they work for it their wages are a first charge which has to be paid before capital gets a penny of interest or profit, and if the failure of the industry is complete the capital sunk in it will be gone.

FOOTNOTES:

[1]

Pages 24, 25.

CHAPTER II

BANKING MACHINERY

Capital, then, is wealth invested in industry, finance is the machinery by which this process of investment is carried out, and international finance is the machinery by which the wealth of one country is invested in another.

Let us consider the case of a doctor in a provincial town who is making an annual income of about £800 a year, living on £600 of it and saving £200. Instead of spending this quarter of his income on immediate enjoyments, such as wine and cigars, and journeys to London, he invests it in different parts of the world through the mechanism of international finance, because he has been attracted by the advantages of a system of investment which was fashionable some years ago, which worked by what was called Geographical Distribution.[2] This meant to say that the investors who practised it put their money into as many different countries as possible, so that the risk of loss owing to climatic or other disturbances might be spread as widely as possible. So here we have this quiet country doctor spreading all over the world the money that he gets for dosing and poulticing and dieting his patients, stimulating industry in many climates and bringing some part of its proceeds to be added to his store. Let us see how the process works. First of all he has a bank, into which he pays day by day the fees that he receives in coin or notes and the cheques that he gets, each half year, from those of his patients who have an account with him. As long as his money is in the bank, the bank has the use of it, and not much of it is likely to go abroad. For the banks use most of the funds entrusted to them in investments in home securities, or in loans and advances to home customers. Part of them they use in buying bills of exchange drawn on London houses by merchants and financiers all over the world, so that even when he pays money into his bank it is possible that our doctor is already forming part of the machinery of international finance and involving us in the need for an explanation of one of its mysteries.

A bill of exchange is an order to pay. When a merchant in Argentina sells wheat to an English buyer, he draws a bill on the buyer (or some bank or firm in England whom the buyer instructs him to draw on), saying, "Pay to me" (or anybody else whom he may name) "the sum of so many pounds." This bill, if it is drawn on a firm or company of well known standing, the seller of the wheat can immediately dispose of, and so has got payment for his goods. Usually the bill is made payable two or three, or sometimes six months after sight, that is after it has been received by the firm on which it is drawn, and "accepted" by it, that is signed across the front to show that the firm drawn on will pay the bill when it falls due. These bills of exchange, when thus accepted, are promises to pay entered into by firms of first-rate standing, and are held as investments by English banks. Bills of exchange are also drawn on English houses to finance trade transactions between foreign countries, and also as a means of borrowing money from England. When they are drawn on behalf of English customers, the credit given is given at home, but as it is (almost always) given in connection with international trade, the transaction may be considered as part of international finance. When they are drawn on behalf of foreign countries, trading with other foreigners, or using the credit to lend to other foreigners, the connection with international finance is obvious. They are readily taken all over the world, because all over the world there are people who have payments to make to England owing to the wide distribution of our trade, and it has long been England's boast that bills of exchange drawn on London firms are the currency of international commerce and finance.

Some people tell us that this commanding position of the English bill in the world's markets is in danger of being lost owing to the present war: in the first place because America is gaining wealth rapidly, while we are shooting away our savings, and also because the Germans will make every endeavour to free themselves from dependence on English credit for the conduct of their trade. Certainly this danger is a real one, but it does not follow that we shall not be able to meet it and defeat it. If the war teaches us to work hard and consume little, so that when peace comes we shall have a great volume of goods to export, there is no reason why the bill on London should not retain much if not all of its old prestige and supremacy in the marts of the world. For we must always remember that finance is only the handmaid of industry. She is often a pert handmaid who steals her mistress's clothes and tries to flaunt before the world as the mistress, and so she sometimes imposes on many people who ought to know better, who think that finance is an all-powerful influence. Finance is a mighty influence, but it is a mere piece of machinery which assists, quickens, and lives on production. The men who make and grow things, and carry them from the place where they are made and grown to the place where they are wanted, these are the men who furnish the raw material of finance, without which it would have to shut up its shop.

If they and their work ceased, we should all starve, and the financiers would have nothing behind the pieces of paper that they handle. If finance and the financiers were suddenly to cease, there would be a very awkward jar and jolt in our commercial machinery, but as long as the stuff and the means of carrying it were available, we should very soon patch up some other method for exchanging it between one nation and another and one citizen and another. The supremacy of the London bill of exchange was created only to a small extent by any supremacy in London's financial machinery; it was based chiefly on the supremacy of England's world-wide trade, and on our readiness to take goods from all nations. The consequence of this was that traders of all nations sold goods to us, and so had claims on us and drew bills on us, and bought goods from us, and so owed us money and wanted to buy bills drawn on us to pay their debts with. So everywhere the bill on London was known and familiar and welcome. If the Americans are able and willing to develop such a world-wide trade as ours, then the bill on New York will have a vogue all over the world just as is enjoyed by the bill on London. Then London and New York will have to fight the matter out by seeing which will provide the best and cheapest machinery for discounting the bill, that is, turning it into cash on arrival, so that the holder of it shall get the best possible price at the present moment, for a bill due two or three months hence.

In this matter of machinery London has certain advantages which ought, if well used and applied, to stand her in good stead in any struggle that lies ahead of her. London's credit machinery has grown up in almost complete freedom from legislation, and it has consequently been able to grow, without let or hindrance, along the lines that expediency and convenience have shown to be most practical and useful. It has been too busy to be logical or theoretical, and consequently it is full of absurdities and anomalies, but it works with marvellous ease and elasticity.

In its centre is the Bank of England, with the prestige of antiquity and of official dignity derived from acting as banker to the British Government, and with still more practical strength derived from acting as banker to all the other great banks, several of them much bigger, in certain respects, than it. The Bank of England is very severely and strictly restricted by law in the matter of its note issue, but it luckily happened, when Parliament was imposing these restrictions on the Bank's business, that note issuing was already becoming a comparatively unimportant part of banking, owing to the development of the use of cheques. Nowadays, when borrowers go to the Bank of England for loans, they do not want to take them out in notes; all they want is a credit in the Bank's books against which they can draw cheques. A credit in the Bank of England's books is regarded by the financial community as "cash," and this pleasant fiction has given the Bank the power of creating cash by a stroke of its pen and to any extent that it pleases, subject only to its own view as to what is prudent and sound business. On p.33 is a specimen of a return that is published each week by the Bank of England, showing its position in two separate accounts with regard to its note issuing business and its banking business: the return taken is an old one, published before the war, so as to show how the machine worked in normal times before war's demands had blown out the balloon of credit to many times its former size.

If the commercial and financial community is short of cash, all that it has to do is to go to the Bank of England and borrow a few millions, and the only effect on the Bank's position is an addition of so many millions to its holding of securities and a similar addition to its deposits. It may sometimes happen that the borrowers may require the use of actual currency, and in that case part of the advances made will be taken out in the form of notes and gold, but as a general rule the Bank is able to perform its function of providing emergency credit by merely making entries in its books.

A BANK RETURN

ISSUE DEPARTMENT.

Notes Issued	£56,908,235	Government Debt	£11,015,100
		Other Securities	7,434,900
		Gold Coin and Bullion	38,458,235
		Silver Bullion	---
	£56,908,235		£56,908,235

BANKING DEPARTMENT.

Proprietors' Capital	£14,553,000	Government Securities	£11,005,126
Rest	3,431,484	Other Securities	33,623,288
Public Deposits	13,318,714	Notes	27,592,980
Other Deposits	42,485,605	Gold and Silver Coin	1,596,419
Seven Day and other			
Bills	29,010		
	£73,817,813		£73,817,813

With the Bank of England thus acting as a centre to the system, there has grown up around it a circle of the great joint stock banks, which provide credit and currency for commerce and finance by lending money and taking it on deposit, or on current account. These banks work under practically no legal restrictions of any kind with regard to the amount of cash that they hold, or the use that they make of the money that is entrusted to their keeping. They are not allowed, if they have an office in London, to issue notes at all, but in all other respects they are left free to conduct their business along the lines that experience has shown them to be most profitable to themselves, and most convenient for their customers. Being joint stock companies they have to publish periodically, for the information of their shareholders, a balance sheet showing their position. Before the war most of them published a monthly statement of their position, but this habit has lately been given up. No legal regulations guide them in the form or extent of the information that they give in their balance sheets, and their great success and solidity is a triumph of unfettered business freedom. This absence of restriction gives great elasticity and adaptability to the credit machinery of London. Here is a specimen of one of their balance sheets, slightly simplified, and dating from the days before the war:—

LIABILITIES.

Capital (subscribed)   £14,000,000

Paid up	3,500,000
Reserve	4,000,000
Deposits	87,000,000
Circular Notes, etc.	3,000,000
Acceptances	6,000,000
Profit and loss	500,000

£104,000,000

ASSETS

Cash in hand and
  at Bank of England   £12,500,000
Cash at call and

- 15 -

short notice	13,000,000
Bills discounted	19,000,000
Govt. Securities	5,000,000
Other Investments	4,500,000
Advances and loans	42,000,000
Liability of customers	
on account of	
Acceptances	6,000,000
Promises	2,000,000

£104,000,000

On one side are the sums that the bank has received, in the shape of capital subscribed, from its shareholders, and in the shape of deposits from its customers, including Dr. Pillman and thousands like him; on the other the cash that it holds, in coin, notes and credit at the Bank of England, its cash lent at call or short notice to bill brokers (of whom more anon) and the Stock Exchange, the bills of exchange that it holds, its investments in British Government and other stocks, and the big item of loans and advances, through which it finances industry and commerce at home. It should be noted that the entry on the left side of the balance sheet, "Acceptances," refers to bills of exchange which the bank has accepted for merchants and manufacturers who are importing goods and raw material, and have instructed the foreign exporters to draw bills on their bankers. As these merchants and manufacturers are responsible to the bank for meeting the bills when they fall due, the acceptance item is balanced by an exactly equivalent entry on the other side, showing this liability of customers as an asset in the bank's favour.

This business of acceptance is done not only by the great banks, but also by a number of private firms with connections in foreign countries, and at home, through which they place their names and credit at the disposal of people less eminent for wealth and position, who pay them a commission for the use of them.

Other wheels in London's credit machinery are the London offices of colonial and foreign banks, and the bill brokers or discount houses which deal in bills of exchange and constitute the discount market. Thus we see that there is in London a highly specialized and elaborate machinery for making and dealing in these bills, which are the currency of international trade. Let us recapitulate the history of the bill and see the part contributed to its career by each wheel in the machine. We imagined a bill drawn by an Argentine seller against a cargo of wheat shipped to an English merchant. The bill will be drawn on a London accepting house, to whom the English merchant is liable for its due payment. The Argentine merchant, having drawn the bill, sells it to the Buenos Ayres branch of a South American bank, formed with English capital, and having its head office in London. It is shipped to London, to the head office of the South American bank, which presents it for acceptance to the accepting house on which it is drawn, and then sells it to a bill broker at the market rate of discount. If the bill is due three months after sight, and is for £2000, and the market rate of discount is 4 per cent. for three months' bills, the present value of the bill is obviously £1980. The bill broker, either at once or later, probably sells the bill to a bank, which holds it as an investment until its due date, by which time the importer having sold the wheat at a profit, pays the money required to meet the bill to his banker and the transaction is closed. Thus by means of the bill the exporter has received immediate payment for his wheat, the importing merchant has been supplied with credit for three months in which to bring home his profit, and the bank which bought the bill has provided itself with an investment such as bankers love, because it has to be met within a short period by a house of first-rate standing.

All this elaborate, but easily working machinery has grown up for the service of commerce. It is true that bills of exchange are often drawn by moneylenders abroad on moneylenders in England merely in order to raise credit, that is to say, to borrow money by means of the London discount market. Sometimes these credits are used for merely speculative purposes, but in the great majority of cases they are wanted for the furtherance of production in the borrowing country. The justification of the English accepting houses, and bill brokers, and banks (in so far as they engage in this business), is the fact that they are assisting trade, and could not live without trade, and that trade if deprived of their services would be gravely inconvenienced and could only resume its present activity by making a new machinery more or less on the same lines. The bill whose imaginary history has been traced, came into being because the drawer had a claim on England through a trade transaction. He was able to sell it to the South American bank only because the bank knew that many other people in Argentina would have to make payments to England and would come to it and ask it for drafts on London, which, by remitting this bill to be sold in London, it would be able to supply. International finance is so often regarded as a machinery by which paper wealth is manufactured out of nothing, that it is very important to remember that all this paper wealth only acquires value by being ultimately based on something that is grown or made and wanted to keep people alive or comfortable, or at least happy in the belief that they have got something that they thought they wanted, or which habit or convention obliged them to possess.

FOOTNOTES:

[2]

All this imaginary picture is of events before the war. At present Dr. Pillman, being a patriotic citizen, is saving much faster than before, and putting every pound that he can save into the hands of the British Government by subscribing to War Loans and buying Exchequer bonds. He is too old to go and do medical work at the front, so he does the next best thing by cutting down his expenses and finding money for the war.

CHAPTER III

INVESTMENTS AND SECURITIES

So far we have only considered what happens to the money of those who save as long as it is left in the hands of their bankers, and we have seen that it is only likely to be employed internationally, if invested by bankers in bills of exchange which form a comparatively small part of their assets. It is true that bankers also invest money in securities, and that some of these are foreign, but here again the proportion invested abroad is so small that we may be reasonably sure that any money left by us in the hands of our bankers will be employed at home.

But in actual practice those who save do not pile up a large balance at their banks. They keep what is called a current account, consisting of amounts paid in in cash or in cheques on other banks or their own bank, and against this account they draw what is needed for their weekly and monthly payments; sometimes, also, they keep a certain amount on deposit account, that is an account on which they can only draw after giving a week's notice or more. On their deposit account they receive interest, on their current account they may in some parts of the country receive interest on the average balance kept. But the deposit account is most often kept by people who have to have a reserve of cash quickly available for business purposes. The ordinary private investor, when he has got a balance at his bank big enough to make him feel comfortable about being able to meet all probable outgoings, puts any money that he may have to spare into some security dealt in on the Stock Exchange, and so securities and the Stock Exchange have to be described and examined next. They are very much to the point, because it is through them that international finance has done most of its work.

Securities, then, are the stocks, shares and bonds which are given to those who put money into companies, or into loans issued by Governments, municipalities and other public bodies. Let us take the Governments and public bodies first, because the securities issued by them are in some ways simpler than those created by companies.

When a Government wants to borrow, it does so because it needs money. The purpose for which it needs it may be to build a railway or canal, or make a harbour, or carry out a land improvement or irrigation scheme, or otherwise work some enterprise by which the power of the country to grow and make things may be increased. Enterprises of this kind are usually called reproductive, and in many cases the actual return from them in cash more than suffices to meet the interest on the debt raised to carry them out, to say nothing of the direct benefit to the country in increasing its output of wealth. In England the Government has practically no debt that is represented by reproductive assets. Our Government has left the development of the country's resources to private enterprise, and the only assets from which it derives a revenue are the Post Office buildings, the Crown lands and some shares in the Suez Canal which were bought for a political purpose. Governments also borrow money because their revenue from taxes is less than the sums that they are spending. This happens most often and most markedly when they are carrying on war, or when nations are engaged in a competition in armaments, building navies or raising armies against one another so as to be ready for war if it happens. This kind of debt is called dead-weight debt, because there is no direct or indirect increase, in consequence of it, in the country's power to produce things that are wanted. This kind of borrowing is generally excused on the ground that provision for the national safety is a matter which concerns posterity quite as much as the present generation, and that it is, therefore, fair to leave posterity to pay part of the bill.

Municipalities likewise borrow both for reproductive purposes and for objects from which no direct revenue can be expected. They may invest money lent them in gas or electric works or water supply or tramways, and get an income from them which will more than pay the interest on the money borrowed. Or they may put it into public parks and recreation grounds or municipal buildings, or improvements in sanitation, thereby beautifying and cleansing the town. If they do these things in such a way as to make the town a pleasanter and healthier place to live in, they may indirectly increase their revenue; but if they do them extravagantly and badly, they run the risk of putting a burden on the ratepayers that will make people shy of living within their borders.

Whatever be the object for which the loan is issued, the procedure is the same by which the money is raised. The Government or municipality invites subscriptions through a bank or through some great financial house, which publishes what is called a prospectus by circular, and in the papers, giving the terms and details of the loan. People who have money to spare, or are able to borrow money from their bankers, and are attracted by the terms of the loan, sign an application form which is issued with the prospectus, and send a cheque for the sum, usually 5 per cent. of the amount that they apply for, which is payable on application. If the loan is over-subscribed, the applicants will only receive part of the sums for which they apply. If it is not fully subscribed, they will get all that they have asked for, and the balance left over will be taken up in most cases by a syndicate formed by the bank or firm that issued the loan, to "underwrite" it. Underwriting means guaranteeing the success of a loan, and those who do so receive a commission of anything from 1 to 3 per cent.; if the loan is popular and goes well the underwriters take their commission and are quit; if the loan is what the City genially describes as a "frost," the underwriters may find themselves saddled with the greater part of it, and will have the pleasure of nursing it until such time as the investing public will take it off their hands. Underwriting is thus a profitable business when times are good, and the public is feeding freely, but it can only be indulged in by folk with plenty of capital or credit, and so able to carry large blocks of stock if they find themselves left with them.

To take a practical example, let us suppose that the King of Ruritania is informed by his Minister of Marine that a battleship must at once be added to its fleet because his next door neighbour is thought to be thinking of making himself stronger on the water, while his Minister of Finance protests that it is impossible, without the risk of serious trouble, to add anything further to the burdens of the taxpayers. A loan is the easy and obvious way out. London and Paris between them will find two or three millions with pleasure. That will be enough for a battleship and something over in the way of new artillery for the army which can be ordered in France so as to secure the consent of the French Government, which was wont to insist that a certain proportion of any loan raised in Paris must be spent in the country. (It need hardly be said that all these events are supposed to be happening in the years before the war.) Negotiations are entered into with a group of French banks and an English issuing house. The French banks take over their share, and sell it to their customers who are, or were, in the habit of following the lead of their bankers in investment with a blind confidence, that gave the French banks enormous power in the international money market. The English issuing house sends round a stockbroker to underwrite the loan. If the issuing house is one that is usually successful in its issues, the privilege of underwriting anything that it brings out is eagerly sought for. Banks, financial firms, insurance companies, trust companies and stockbrokers with big investment connections will take as much underwriting as they are offered, in many cases without making very searching inquiry into the terms of the security offered. The name of the issuing house and the amount of the underwriting commission —which we will suppose in this case to be 2 per cent.—is enough for them. They know that if they refuse any chance of underwriting that is offered, they are not likely to get a chance when the next loan comes out, and since underwriting is a profitable business for those who can afford to run its risks, many firms put their names down for anything that is put before them, as long as they have confidence in the firm that is handling the loan. This power in the hands of the big issuing houses, to get any loan that they choose to father underwritten in a few hours by a crowd of eager followers, gives them, of course, enormous strength and lays a heavy responsibility on them. They only preserve it by being careful in the use of it, and exercising great discrimination in the class of securities that they handle.

While the underwriting is going on the prospectus is being prepared by which the subscriptions of the public are invited, and in the meantime it will probably happen that the newspapers have had a hint that a Ruritanian loan is on the anvil, so that preliminary paragraphs may prepare an atmosphere of expectancy. News of a forthcoming new issue is always a welcome item in the dull routine of a City article, and the journalists are only serving their public and their papers in being eager to chronicle it. Lurid stories are still handed down by City tradition of how great City journalists acquired fortunes in days gone by, by being allotted blocks of new loans so that they might expand on their merits and then sell them at a big profit when they had created a public demand for them. There seems to be no doubt that this kind of thing used to happen in the dark ages when finance and City journalism did a good deal of dirty business between them. Now, the City columns of the great daily papers have for a very long time been free from any taint of this kind, and on the whole it may be said that finance is a very much cleaner affair than either law or politics. It is true that swindles still happen in the City, but their number is trivial compared with the volume of the public's money that is handled and invested. It is only in the by-ways of finance and in the gutters of City journalism that the traps are laid for the greedy and gullible public, and if the public walks in, it has itself to blame. A genuine investor who wants security and a safe return on his money can always get it. Unfortunately the investor is almost always at the same time a speculator, and is apt to forget the distinction; and those who ask for a high rate of interest, absolute safety and a big rise in the prices of securities that they buy are only inviting disaster by the greed that wants the unattainable and the gullibility that deludes them into thinking they can have it.

To return to our Ruritanian loan, which we left being underwritten. The prospectus duly comes out and is advertised in the papers and sown broadcast over the country through the post. It offers £1,500,000 (part of £3,000,000 of which half is reserved for issue in Paris), 4-1/2 per cent. bonds of the Kingdom of Ruritania, with interest payable on April 1st and October 1st, redeemable by a cumulative Sinking Fund of 1 per cent., operating by annual drawings at par, the price of issue being 97, payable as to 5 per cent. on application, 15 per cent. on allotment and the balance in instalments extending over four months. Coupons and drawn bonds are payable in sterling at the countinghouse of the issuing firm. The extent of the other information given varies considerably. Some firms rely so far on their own prestige and the credit of those on whose account they offer loans, that they state little more than the bare terms of the issue as given above. Others deign to give details concerning the financial position of the borrowing Government, such as its revenue and expenditure for a term of years, the amount of its outstanding debt, and of its assets if any. If the credit of the Kingdom of Ruritania is good, such a loan as here described would be, or would have been before the war, an attractive issue, since the investor would get a good rate of interest for his money, and would be certain of getting par or £100, some day, for each bond for which he now pays £97. This is ensured by the action of the Sinking Fund of 1 per cent. cumulative, which works as follows. Each year, as long as the loan is outstanding the Kingdom of Ruritania will have to put £165,000 in the hands of the issuing houses, to be applied to interest and Sinking Fund. In the first year interest at 4-1/2 per cent. will take £135,000 and Sinking Fund (1 per cent. of £3,000,000) £30,000; this £30,000 will be applied to the redemption of bonds to that value, which are drawn by lot; so that next year the interest charge will be less and the amount available for Sinking Fund will be greater; and each year the comfortable effect of this process continues, until at last the whole loan is redeemed and every investor will have got his money back and something over. The effect of this obligation to redeem, of course, makes the market in the loan very steady, because the chance of being drawn at par in any year, and the certainty of being drawn if the investor holds it long enough, ensures that the market price will be strengthened by this consideration.

Such being the terms of the loan we may be justified in supposing—if Ruritania has a clean record in its treatment of its creditors, and if the issuing firm is one that can be relied on to do all that can be done to safeguard their interests, that the loan is a complete success and is fully subscribed for by the public. The underwriters will consequently be relieved of all liability and will pocket their 2 per cent., which they have earned by guaranteeing the success of the issue. If some financial or political shock had occurred which made investors reluctant to put money into anything at the time when the prospectus appeared or suggested the likelihood that Ruritania might be involved in war, then the underwriters would have had to take up the greater part of the loan and pay for it out of their own pockets; and this is the risk for which they are given their commission. Ruritania will have got its money less the cost of underwriting, advertising, commissions, 1 per cent. stamp payable to the British Government, and the profit of the issuing firm. Some shipyard in the north will lay down a battleship and English shareholders and workmen will benefit by the contract, and the investors will have got well secured bonds paying them a good rate of interest and likely to be easily saleable in the market if the holders want to turn them into cash. The bonds will be large pieces of paper stating that they are 4-1/2 per cent. bonds of the Kingdom of Ruritania for £20, £100, £500 or £1000 as the case may be, and they will each have a sheet of coupons attached, that is, small pieces to be cut off and presented at the date of each interest payment; each one states the amount due each half year and the date when it will have to be met.

Bonds are called bearer securities, that is to say, possession of them entitles the bearer to receive payment of them when drawn and to collect the coupons at their several dates. They are the usual form for the debts of foreign Governments and municipalities, and of foreign railway and industrial companies.

In England we chiefly affect what are called registered and inscribed stocks— that is, if our Government or one of our municipalities issues a loan, the subscribers have their names registered in a book by the debtor, or its banker, and merely hold a certificate which is a receipt, but the possession of which is not in itself evidence of ownership. There are no coupons, and the half-yearly interest is posted to stockholders, or to their bankers or to any one else to whom they may direct it to be sent. Consequently when the holder sells it is not enough for him to hand over his certificate, as is the case with a bearer security, but the stock has to be transferred into the name of the buyer in the register kept by the debtor, or by the bank which manages the business for it.

When the securities offered are not loans by public bodies, but represent an interest in a company formed to build a railway or carry on any industrial or agricultural or mining enterprise, the procedure will be on the same lines, except that the whole affair will be on a less exalted plane. Such an issue would not, save in exceptional circumstances, as when a great railway is offering bonds or debenture stock, be fathered by one of the leading financial firms. Industrial ventures are associated with so many risks that they are usually left to the smaller fry, and those who underwrite them expect higher rates of commission, while subscribers can only be tempted by anticipations of more mouth-filling rates of interest or profit. This distinction between interest and profit brings us to a further difference between the securities of companies and public bodies. Public bodies do not offer profit, but interest, and the distinction is very important. A Government asks for your money and promises to pay a rate for it, whether the object on which the money is spent be profit-earning or no, and, if it is, whether a profit be earned or no. A company asks subscribers to buy it up and become owners of it, taking its profits, that it expects to earn, and getting no return at all on their money if its business is unfortunate and the profits never make their appearance. Consequently the shareholders in a company run all the risks that industrial enterprise is heir to, and the return, if any, that comes into their pockets depends on the ability of the enterprise to earn profits over and above all that it has to pay for raw material, wages and other working expenses, all of which have to be met before the shareholder gets a penny.

In order to meet the objections of steady-going investors to the risks involved by thus becoming industrial adventurers, a system has grown up by which the capital of companies is subdivided into securities that rank ahead of one another. Companies issue debts, like public bodies, in the shape of bonds or debenture stocks, which entitle the holders of them to a stated rate of interest, and no more, and are often repayable at a due date, by drawings or otherwise. These are the first charge on the concern after wages and other working expenses have been paid, and the shareholders do not get any profit until the interest on the company's debt has been met. Further, the actual capital held by the shareholders is generally divided into two classes, preference and ordinary, of which the preference take a fixed rate before the ordinary shareholders get anything, and the ordinary shareholders take the whole of any balance left over. Sometimes, the preference holders have a right to further participation after the ordinary have received a certain amount of dividend, or share of profit, and there are almost endless variations of the manner in which the different classes of holders may claim to divide the profits, by means of preference, preferred, ordinary, preferred ordinary, deferred ordinary, founders' shares, management shares, etc., etc.

All these variations in the position of the shareholder, however, do not alter the great essential difference between him and the creditor, the man who lends money to a Government or enterprise with a fixed rate of interest, and, in most cases, a claim for repayment sooner or later. The shareholder, whether preference or ordinary, puts his money into a venture with no claim for repayment, unless the company is wound up, in which case his claim ranks, of course, after that of every creditor. If he wants to get his money out again he can only do so by selling his stock or shares at any price that they will fetch in the stock market.

Thus, if we take as an example a Brewery company with a total debt and capital of three millions, we may suppose that it will have a million 4-1/2 per cent, debenture stock, entitling the creditors who own it to interest at that rate, and repayment in 1935, a million of 6 per cent. cumulative preference stock, giving holders a fixed dividend, if earned, of 6 per cent, which dividend and all arrears have to be paid before the ordinary shareholders get anything, and a million in ordinary shares of £10 each, whose holders take any balance that may be left. This is the total of the money that has been received from the public when the company was floated and put into the brewery plant, tied houses, or other assets out of which the company makes its revenue.

These bonds and stocks and shares are the machinery of international finance, by which moneylenders of one nation provide borrowers in others with the wherewithal to carry out enterprises, or make payments for which they have not cash available at home. It was shown in a previous chapter that bills of exchange are a means by which the movements of commodities from market to market are financed, and the gap in time is bridged between production and consumption. Stock Exchange securities are more permanent investments, put into industry for longer periods or for all time. Midway between them are securities such as Treasury bills with which Governments raise the wind for a time, pending the collection of revenue, and the one or two years' notes with which American railroads lately financed themselves for short periods, in the hope that the conditions for an issue of bonds with longer periods to run, might become more favourable.

So far we have only considered the machinery by which these securities are created and issued to the public, but it must not be supposed that investment is only possible when new securities are being offered. Many investors have a prejudice against ever buying a new security, preferring those which have a record and a history behind them, and buying them in the market whenever they have money to invest. This market is the Stock Exchange in which securities of all kinds and of all countries are dealt in. Following the history of the Ruritanian loan, we may suppose that it will be dealt in regularly in that section of the Stock Exchange in which the loans of Foreign Governments are marketed. Any original subscriber who wants to turn his bonds into money can do so by instructing his broker to sell them; anyone who wants to do so can acquire a holding in them by a purchase. The terms on which they will be bought or sold will depend on the variations in the demand for, and supply of, them. If a number of holders want to sell, either because they want cash for other purposes, or because they are nervous about the political outlook, or because they think that money is going to be scarce and so there will be better opportunities for investment later on, then the price will droop. But if the political sky is serene and people are saving money fast and investing it in Stock Exchange securities, then the price will go up and those who want to buy it will pay more. The price of all securities, as of everything else, depends on the extent to which people who have not got them demand them, in relation to the extent to which those who have got them are ready to part with them. Price is ultimately a question of what people think about things, and this is why the fluctuations in the price of Stock Exchange securities are so incalculable and often so irrational. If a sufficient number of misguided people with money in their pockets think that a bad security is worth buying they will put the price of it up in the face of the logic of facts and all the arguments of reason. These wild fluctuations, of course, take place chiefly in the more speculative securities. Shares in a gold mine can go to any price that the credulity of buyers dictates, since there is no limit to the amount of gold that people can imagine to be under the ground in its territory.

All the Stock Exchanges of the world are in communication with one another by telegraph, or telephone, and so their feelings about prices react on one another's nerves and imaginations, and the Stock Exchange price list may be said to be the language of international finance, as the bill of exchange is its currency.

CHAPTER IV

FINANCE AND TRADE

We have seen that finance becomes international when capital goes abroad, by being lent by investors in one country to borrowers in another, or by being invested in enterprises formed to carry on some kind of business abroad. We have next to consider why capital goes abroad and whether it is a good or a bad thing, for it to do so.

Capital goes abroad because it is more wanted in other countries than in the country of its origin, and consequently those who invest abroad are able to do so to greater advantage. In countries like England and France, where there have been for many centuries thrifty folk who have saved part of their income, and placed their savings at the disposal of industry, it is clear that industry is likely to be better supplied with capital than in the new countries which have been more lately peopled, and in which the store of accumulated goods is less adequate to the industrial needs of the community. For we must always remember that though we usually speak and think of capital as so much money it is really goods and property. In England money consists chiefly of credit in the books of banks, which can only be created because there is property on which the banks can make advances, or because there is property expressed in securities in which the banks can invest or against which they can lend. Because our forefathers did not spend all their incomes on their own personal comfort and amusement but put a large part of them into railways and factories, and shipbuilding yards, our country is now reasonably well supplied with the machinery of production and the means of transport. Whether it might not be much better so equipped is a question with which we are not at present concerned. At least it may be said that it is more fully provided in these respects than new countries like our colonies, America and Argentina, or old countries like Russia and China in which industrial development is a comparatively late growth, so that there has been less time for the storing up, by saving, of the necessary machinery.

So it comes about that new countries are in greater need of capital than old ones and consequently are ready to pay a higher rate of interest for it to lenders or to tempt shareholders with a higher rate of profit. And so the opportunity is given to investors in England to develop the agricultural or industrial resources of all the countries under the sun to their own profit and to that of the countries that it supplies. When, for example, the Government of one of the Australian colonies came to London to borrow money for a railway, it said in effect to English investors, "Your railways at home have covered your country with such a network that there are no more profitable lines to be built. The return that you get from investing in them is not too attractive in view of all the trade risks to which they are subject. Do not put your money into them, but lend it to us. We will take it and build a railway in a country which wants them, and, whether the railway pays or no, you will be creditors of a Colonial Government with the whole wealth of the colony pledged to pay you interest and pay back your money when the loan falls due for repayment." For in Australia the railways have all been built by the Colonial Governments, partly because they wished, by pledging their collective credit, to get the money as cheaply as possible, and keep the profits from them in their own hands, and partly probably because they did not wish the management of their railways to be in the hands of London boards. In Argentina, on the other hand, the chief railways have been built, not by the Government but by English companies, shareholders in which have taken all the risks of the enterprise, and have thereby secured handsome profits to themselves, tempered with periods of bad traffic and poor returns.

For many years there was a good deal of prejudice in England against investing abroad, especially among the more sleepy classes of investors who had made their money in home trade, and liked to keep it there when they invested it. As traders, we learnt a world-wide outlook many centuries before we did so as investors. To send a ship with a cargo of English goods to a far off country to be exchanged into its products was a risk that our enterprising forefathers took readily. The ship took in its return cargo and came home, bringing its sheaves with it in a reasonable time, though the Antonios of the period sometimes had awkward moments if their ships were delayed by bad weather, and they were liable on a bond to Shylock. But it was quite another matter to lend money in a distant country when communication was slow and difficult, and social and political conditions had not gained the stability that is needed before contracts can be entered into extending over many years. International moneylending took place, of course, in the middle ages, and everybody knows Motley's great description of the consternation that shook Europe when Philip the Second repudiated his debts "to put an end to such financiering and unhallowed practices with bills of exchange."[3] But though there were moneylenders in those days who obliged foreign potentates with loans, the business was in the hands of expert professional specialists, and there was no medieval counterpart of the country doctor whom we have imagined to be developing industry all over the world by placing his savings in foreign countries. There could be no investing public until there were large classes that had accumulated wealth by saving, and until the discovery of the principle of limited liability enabled adventurers to put their savings into industry without running the risk of losing not only what they put in, but all else that they possessed. By means of this system, the risk of a shareholder in a company is limited to a definite amount, usually the amount that has been paid up on his shares or stock, though in some cases, such as bank and insurance shares, there is a further reserve liability which is left for the protection of the companies' customers.

In the eighteenth century a great outburst of gambling in the East Indian and South Sea companies, and a horde of less notorious concerns was a short-lived episode which must have helped for a very long time to strengthen the natural prejudice that investors feel in favour of putting their money into enterprise at home; and it was still further strengthened by the disastrous results of another great plague of bad foreign securities that smote London just after the war that ended at Waterloo. This prejudice survived up to within living memory, and I have heard myself old-fashioned stockbrokers maintain that, after all, there was no investment like Home Rails, because investors could always go and look at their property, which could not run away. Gradually, however, the habit of foreign investment grew, under the influence of the higher rates of interest and profit offered by new countries, the greater political stability that was developed in them, and political apprehensions at home. In fact it grew so fast and so lustily that there came a time, not many years ago, when investments at home were under a cloud, and many clients, when asking their brokers where and how to place their savings, stipulated that they must be put somewhere abroad.

This was at a time when Mr. Lloyd George's financial measures were arousing resentment and fear among the investing classes, and when preachers of the Tariff Reform creed were laying so much stress on our "dying industries" that they were frightening those who trusted them into the belief that the sun was setting on our industrial greatness. The effect of this belief was to bring down the prices of home securities, and to raise those of other countries, as investors changed from the former into the latter.

So the theory that we were industrially and financially doomed got another argument from its own effects, and its missionaries were able to point to the fall in Consols and the relative steadiness of foreign and colonial securities which their own preaching had brought about, as fresh evidence of its truth. At the same time fear of Socialistic legislation at home had the humorous result of making British investors fear to touch Consols, but rush eagerly to buy the securities of Colonial Governments which had gone much further in the direction of Socialism than we had. Those were great days for all who handled the machinery of oversea investment and in the last few years before the war it is estimated that England was placing some 200 millions a year in her colonies and dependencies and in foreign countries. Old-fashioned folk who still believed in the industrial strength and financial stability of their native land waited for the reaction which was bound to follow when some of the countries into which we poured capital so freely, began to find a difficulty in paying the interest; and just before the war this reaction began to happen, in consequence of the default in Mexico and the financial embarrassments of Brazil. Mexico had shown that the political stability which investors had believed it to have achieved was a very thin veneer and a series of revolutions had plunged that hapless land into anarchy. Brazil was suffering from a heavy fall in the price of one of her chief staple products, rubber, owing to the competition of plantations in Ceylon, Straits Settlements and elsewhere, and was finding difficulty in meeting the interest on the big load of debt that the free facilities given by English and French investors had encouraged her to pile up. She had promised retrenchment at home, and another big loan was being hatched to tide her over her difficulties—or perhaps increase them—when the war cloud began to gather and she has had to resort for the second time in her history to the indignity of a funding scheme. By this "new way of paying old debts" she does not pay interest to her bondholders in cash, but gives them promises to pay instead, and so increases the burden of her debt, which she hopes some day to be able to shoulder again, by resuming payments in cash.

Mexico and Brazil were not the only countries that were showing signs, in 1914, of having indulged too freely in the opportunities given them by the eagerness of English and French investors to place money abroad. It looked as if in many parts of the earth a time of financial disillusionment was dawning, the probable result of which would have been a strong reaction in favour of investment at home. Then came the war with a short sharp spell of financial chaos followed by a halcyon period for young countries, which enabled them to sell their products at greatly increased prices to the warring powers and so to meet their debt charges with an ease that they had never dreamt of, and even to find themselves lending, out of the abundance of their war profits, money to their creditors. America has led the way with a loan of £100 millions to France and England, and Canada has placed 10 millions of credit at the disposal of the Mother Country. There can be little doubt that if the war goes on, and the neutral countries continue to pile up profits by selling food and war materials to the belligerents, many of them will find it convenient to lend some of their gains to their customers. America has also been taking the place of France and England as international moneylenders by financing Argentina; and a great company has been formed in New York to promote international activity, on the part of Americans, in foreign countries. "And thus the whirligig of time," assisted by the eclipse of civilization in Europe, "brings in his revenges" and turns debtors into creditors. In the meantime it need hardly be said that investment at home has become for the time being a matter of patriotic duty for every Englishman, since the financing of the war has the first and last claim on his savings.

Our present concern, however, is not with the war problems of to-day, but with the processes of international finance in the past, and perhaps, before we get to the end, with some attempt to hazard a glimpse into its arrangements in the future. What was the effect on England, and on the countries to whom she lent, of her moneylending activity in the past? As soon as we begin to look into this question we see once more how close is the connection between finance and trade, and that finance is powerless unless it is supported and in fact made possible by industrial or commercial activity behind it. England's international trade made her international finance possible and necessary. A country can only lend money to others if it has goods and services to supply, for in fact it lends not money but goods and services.

In the beginnings of international trade the older countries exchange their products for the raw materials and food produced by the new ones. Then, as emigrants from the old countries go out into the new ones, they want to be supplied with the comforts and appliances of the older civilizations, such as, to take an obvious example, railways. But as the productions of the new countries, at their early stage of development, do not suffice to pay for all the material and machinery needed for building railways, they borrow, in effect, these materials, in the expectation that the railways will open out their resources, enable them to put more land under the plough and bring more stuff to the seaboard, to be exchanged for the products of Europe. The new country, New Zealand or Japan, or whichever it may be, raises a loan in England for the purpose of building a railway, but it does not take the money raised by the loan in the form of money, but in the form of goods needed for the railway, and sometimes in the form of the services of those who plan and build it. It does not follow that all the stuff and services needed for the enterprise are necessarily bought in the country that lends the money; for instance, if Japan borrows money from us for a railway, she may buy some of the steel rails and locomotives in Belgium, and instruct us to pay Belgium for her purchases. If so, instead of sending goods to Japan we shall have to send goods or services to Belgium, or pay Belgium with the claim on some other country that we have established by sending goods or services to it. But, however long the chain may be, the practical fact is that when we lend money we lend somebody the right to claim goods or services from us, whether they are taken from us by the borrower, or by somebody to whom the borrower gives a claim on us.

If, whenever we made a loan, we had to send the money to the borrower in the form of gold, our gold store would soon be used up, and we should have to leave off lending. In other words, our financiers would have to retire from business very quickly if it were not that our manufacturers and shipowners and all the rest of our industrial army produced the goods and services to meet the claims on our industry given, or rather lent, to other countries by the machinery of finance.

This obvious truism is often forgotten by those who look on finance as an independent influence that can make money power out of nothing; and those who forget it are very likely to find themselves entangled in a maze of error. We can make the matter a little clearer if we go back to the original saver, whose money, or claims on industry, is handled by the professional financier. Those who save do so by going without things. Instead of spending their earnings on immediate enjoyment they spend part of them in providing somebody else with goods that they need, and taking from that somebody else an annual payment for the use of these goods for a certain period, after which, if it is a case of a loan, the transaction is closed by repayment of the advance, which again is effected by a transfer of goods. When our country doctor subscribes to an Australian loan raised by a colony for building a railway, he hands over to the colony money which a less thrifty citizen would have spent on pleasures and amusements, and the colony uses it to buy railway material. Thus in effect the doctor is spending his money in making a railway in Australia. He is induced to do so by the promise of the colony to give him £4 every year for each £100 that he lends. If there were not enough people like him to put money into industry instead of spending it on themselves, there could be no railway building or any other form of industrial growth. It is often contended that a reconstruction of society on a Socialistic basis would abolish the capitalist; but in fact it would make everybody a capitalist because the State would have to make the citizens as a whole go without certain immediate enjoyments and work on the production of the machinery of industry. Instead of saving being left to the individual and rewarded by a rate of interest, it would be imposed on all and rewarded by a greater productive power, and consequent increase in commodities, enjoyed by the community and distributed among all its members. The advantages, on paper, of such an arrangement over the present system are obvious. Whether they would be equally obvious in practice would depend on the discretion with which the Government handled the enormous responsibility placed in its hands. But the essential fact that capital can only be got by being saved, and earns the reward that it gets, would remain as strongly in force as ever, and will do so until we have learnt to make goods out of nothing and without effort.

Going back to our doctor, who lends railway material to an Australian colony, we see that every year for each £100 lent the colony has to send him £4. This it can only do if its mines and fields and factories can turn out metals or wheat or wool, or other goods which can be shipped to England or elsewhere and be sold, so that the doctor's £4 is provided. And so though on both sides the transaction is expressed in money it is in fact carried out in goods, both when the loan is made and the interest is paid. And finally when the loan is paid back again, the colony must have sold goods to provide repayment, unless it meets its debts by raising another. But when a loan is well spent on a railway that is needed for the development of a fertile or productive district, it justifies itself by cheapening transport and quickening the output of wealth in such a manner, that the increased volume of goods that it has helped to create easily meets the interest due to lenders, provides a fund for its redemption at maturity, and leaves the borrower better off, with a more fully equipped productive system.

Since, then, there is this close and obvious connection between finance and trade, it is inevitable that all who partake in the activities of international finance should find their trade quickened by it. England has lent money abroad because she is a great producer, and certain classes of Englishmen are savers, so that there was a balance of goods available for export, to be lent to other countries. In the early years of the nineteenth century, when our industrial power was first beginning to gather strength, we used regularly to export goods to a greater value than we imported. These were the goods that we were lending abroad, clearly showing themselves in our trade ledger. Since then the account has been complicated by the growth of the amount that our debtors owe us every year for interest, and by the huge earnings of our merchant navy, which other countries pay by shipping goods to us, so that, by the growth of these items, the trade balance sheet has been turned in the other direction, and in spite of our lending larger and larger amounts all over the world we now have a balance of goods coming in. Interest due to us and shipping freights and the commissions earned by our bankers and insurance companies were estimated before the war to amount to something like 350 millions a year, so that we were able to lend other countries some 200 millions or more in a year and still take from them a very large balance in goods. After the war this comfortable state of affairs will have been modified by the sales that we are making now in New York of the American Railroad bonds and shares that represented the savings that we had put into America in former years, and by the extent of our war borrowings in America, and elsewhere, if we widen the circle of our creditors. The effect of this will be that we shall owe America for interest on the money that it is lending us, and that it will owe us less interest, owing to the blocks of its securities that it is buying back. Against this we shall be able to set debts due to us from our Allies, but if our borrowings and sales of securities exceed our lendings as the war goes on, we shall thereby be poorer. Our power as a creditor country will be less, until by hard work and strict saving we have restored it. This we can very quickly do, if we remember and apply the lessons that war is teaching us about the number of people able to work, whose capacity was hitherto left fallow, that this country contained, and also about the ease with which we can dispense, when a great crisis makes us sensible, with many of the absurdities and futilities on which much of our money, and productive capacity, used to be wasted.

FOOTNOTES:

[3]

"United Netherlands," chap. xxxii.

CHAPTER V

THE BENEFITS OF INTERNATIONAL FINANCE

When once we have recognized how close is the connection between finance and trade, we have gone a long way towards seeing the greatness of the service that finance renders to mankind, whether it works at home or abroad. At home we owe our factories and our railways and all the marvellous equipment of our power to make things that are wanted, to the quiet, prosaic, and often rather mean and timorous people who have saved money for a rainy day, and put it into industry instead of into satisfying their immediate wants and cravings for comfort and enjoyment It is equally, perhaps still more, true, that we owe them to the brains and energy of those who have planned and organized the equipment of industry, and the thews and sinews of those who have done the heavy work. But brain and muscle would have been alike powerless if there had not been saving folk who lent them raw material, and provided them with the means of livelihood in the interval between the beginning of an industry and the day when its product is sold and paid for.

Abroad, the work of finance has been even more advantageous to mankind, for since it has been shown that international finance is a necessary part of the machinery of international trade, it follows that all the benefits, economic and other, which international trade has wrought for us, are inseparably and inevitably bound up with the progress of international finance. If we had never fertilized the uttermost parts of the earth by lending them money and sending them goods in payment of the sums lent, we never could have enjoyed the stream that pours in from them of raw material and cheap food which has sustained our industry, fed our population, and given us a standard of general comfort such as our forefathers could never have imagined. It is true that at the same time we have benefited others, besides our own customers and debtors. We have opened up the world to trade and other countries reap an advantage by being able to use the openings that we have made. It is sometimes argued that we have in fact merely made the paths of our competitors straight, and that by covering Argentina with a network of railways and so enormously increasing its power to grow things and so to buy things, we have been making an opportunity for German shipbuilders to send liners to the Plate and for German manufacturers to undersell ours with cheap hardware and cotton goods. This is, undoubtedly, true. The great industrial expansion of Germany between 1871 and 1914, has certainly been helped by the paths opened for it all over the world by English trade and finance; and America, our lusty young rival, that is gaining so much strength from the war in which Europe is weakening itself industrially and financially, will owe much of the ease of her prospective expansion to spade-work done by the sleepy Britishers. It may almost be said that we and France as the great providers of capital to other countries have made a world-wide trade possible on its present scale. The work we have done for our own benefit has certainly helped others, but it does not, therefore, follow that it has damaged us.

Looking at the matter from a purely business point of view, we see that the great forward movement in trade and finance that we have led and fostered, has helped us even by helping our rivals. In the first place, it gives us a direct benefit as the owners of the mightiest fleet of merchant ships that the world has seen. We do nearly half the world's carrying trade, and so have reason to rejoice when other nations send goods to the ports that we have opened. By our eminence in finance and the prestige of a bill of exchange drawn on London, we have also supplied the credit by which goods have been paid for in the country of their origin, and nursed until they have come to the land in which they are wanted, and even until the day when they have been turned into a finished product and passed into the hands of the final consumer. But there is also the indirect advantage that we gain, as a nation of producers and financiers, from the growing wealth of other nations. The more wealthy they grow, the more goods they produce want to sell to us, and they cannot sell to us unless they likewise buy from us. If we helped Germany to grow rich, we also helped her to become one of our best customers and so to help us to grow rich. Trade is nothing but an exchange of goods and services. Other countries are not so philanthropic as to kill our trade by making us presents of their products and from the strictly economic point of view, it pays us to see all the world, which is our market, a thriving hive of industry eager to sell us as as it can. It may be that as other countries, with the help of our capital and example, develop industries in which we have been pre-eminent, they may force us to supply them with services of which we are less proud to be the producers. If, for example, the Americans were to drive us out of the neutral markets with their cotton goods, and then spent their profits by revelling in our hotels and thronging out theatres and shooting in Highland deer forests, and buying positions in English society for their daughters we should feel that the course of industry might still be profitable to us, but that it was less satisfactory. On the other hand, it would be absurd for us to expect the rest of the world to stand still industrially in order that we may make profits from producing things for it that it is quite able to make for itself.

For the present we are concerned with the benefits of international finance, which have been shown to begin with its enormous importance as the handmaid of international trade. Trade between nations is desirable for exactly the same reason as trade between one man and another, namely, that each is, naturally or otherwise, better fitted to grow or make certain things, and so an exchange is to their mutual advantage. If this is so, as it clearly is, in the case of two men living in the same street, it is evidently very much more so in the case of two peoples living in different climates and on different soils, and so each of them, by the nature of their surroundings, able to make and grow things that are impossible to the other. English investors, by developing the resources of other countries, through the machinery of international finance, enable us to sit at home in this inclement isle, and enjoy the fruits of tropical skies and soils. It may be true that if they had not done so we should have developed the resources of our own country more thoroughly, using it less as a pleasure ground, and more as a farm and kitchen garden, and that we should have had a larger number of our own folk working for us under our own sky. Instead of thriving on the produce of foreign climes and foreign labour that comes to us to pay interest, we should have lived more on home-made stuff and had more healthy citizens at work on our soil. On the other hand, we should have been hit hard by bad seasons and we should have enjoyed a much less diversified diet. As it is, we take our tea and tobacco and coffee and sugar and wine and oranges and bananas and cheap bread and meat, all as a matter of course, but we could never have enjoyed them if international trade had not brought them to our shores, and if international finance had not quickened and cheapened their growth and transport and marketing. International trade and finance, if given a free hand, may be trusted to bring about, between them, the utmost possible development of the power of the world to grow and make things in the places where they can be grown and made most cheaply and abundantly, in other words, to secure for human effort, working on the available raw material, the greatest possible harvest as the reward of its exertions.

All this is very obvious and very material, but international finance does much more, for it is a great educator and a mighty missionary of peace and goodwill between nations. This also is obvious on a moment's reflection, but it will be rejected as a flat mis-statement by many whose opinion is entitled to respect, and who regard international finance as a bloated spider which sits in the middle of a web of intrigue and chicanery, enticing hapless mankind into its toils and battening on bloodshed and war. So clear-headed a thinker as Mr. Philip Snowden publicly expressed the view not long ago that "the war was the result of secret diplomacy carried on by diplomatists who had conducted foreign policy in the interests of militarists and financiers,"[4] Now Mr. Snowden may possibly be right in his view that the war was produced by diplomacy of the kind that he describes, but with all deference I submit that he is wholly wrong if he thinks that the financiers, as financiers, wanted war either here or in Germany or anywhere else. If they wanted war it was because they believed, rightly or wrongly, that their country had to fight for its existence, or for something equally well worth fighting for, and so as patriotic citizens, they accepted or even welcomed a calamity that could only cause them, as financiers, the greatest embarrassment and the chance of ruin. War has benefited the working classes, and enabled them to take a long stride forward, which we must all hope they will maintain, towards the improvement in their lot which is so long overdue. It has helped the farmers, put fortunes in the pockets of the shipowners, and swollen the profits of any manufacturers who have been able to turn out stuff wanted for war or for the indirect needs of war. The industrial centres are bursting with money, and the greater spending power that has been diffused by war expenditure has made the cheap jewellery trade a thriving industry and increased the consumption of beer and spirits in spite of restrictions and the absence of men at the front. Picture palaces are crammed nightly, furs and finery have had a wonderful season, any one who has a motor car to sell finds plenty of ready buyers, and second-hand pianos are an article that can almost be "sold on a Sunday." But in the midst of this roar of humming trade, finance, and especially international finance, lies stricken and still gasping from the shock of war. When war comes, the price of all property shrivels. This was well known to Falstaff, who, when he brought the news of Hotspur's rebellion, said "You may buy land now as cheap as stinking mackerel," To most financial institutions, this shrivelling process in the price of their securities and other assets, brings serious embarrassment, for there is no corresponding decline in their liabilities, and if they have not founded themselves on the rock of severest prudence in the past, their solvency is likely to be imperilled. Finance knew that it must suffer. The story has often been told, and though never officially confirmed, it has at least the merit of great probability, that in 1911 when the Morocco crisis made a European war probable, the German Government was held back by the warning of its financiers that war would mean Germany's ruin. It is more than likely that a similar warning was given in July, 1914, but that the war party brushed it aside. And now that war is upon us, we are being warned that high finance is intriguing for peace. Mr. Edgar Crammond, a distinguished economist and statistician, published an article in the *Nineteenth Century* of September, 1915, entitled "High Finance and a Premature Peace," calling attention to this danger and urging the need for guarding against it. First too bellicose and now too pacific, High Finance is buffeted and spat upon by men of peace and men of war with a unanimity that must puzzle it. It can hardly err on both sides, but of the two accusers I think that Mr. Crammond is much more likely to be right. But my own personal opinion is that both these accusers are mistaken, that the financiers never wanted war, that if (which I beg to doubt) diplomacy conducted in their interests produced the war, that was because diplomacy misunderstood and bungled their interests, and that now that the war is upon us, the financiers, though all their interests urge them to want peace, would never be parties to intrigues for a peace that was premature or ill-judged.

Perhaps I have a weakness for financiers, but if so it is entitled to some respect, because it is based on closer knowledge of them than is owned by most of their critics. For years it was my business as a City journalist, to see them day by day; and this daily intercourse with financiers has taught me that the popular delusion that depicts them as hard, cruel, ruthless men, living on the blood and sweat of humanity, and engulfed to their eyebrows in their own sordid interests, is about as absurd a hallucination as the stage Irishman. Financiers are quite human—quiet, mild, good-natured people as a rule, many of them spending much time and trouble on good works in their leisure hours. What they want as financiers is plenty of good business and as little as possible disturbance in the orderly course of affairs. Such a cataclysm as the present war could only terrify them, especially those with interests in every country of the world. When war comes, especially such a war as this, financing in its ordinary and most profitable sense has to put up its shutters. Nobody can come to London now for loans except the British, or French, Governments, or, occasionally, one of our colonies. Any other borrower is warned off the field by a ruthless Committee whose leave has to be granted before dealings in new securities are allowed on the Stock Exchange. But when the British Government borrows, there are no profits for the rank and file of financiers. No underwriting is necessary, and the business is carried out by the Bank of England. The commissions earned by brokers are smaller, and the whole City feels that this is no time for profit-making, but for hard and ill-paid work, with depleted staffs, to help the great task of financing a great war. The Stock Exchange is half empty and nearly idle. It is tied and bound by all sorts of regulations in its dealings, and its members have probably suffered as severely from the war as any section of the community. The first interest of the City is unquestionably peace; and the fact that the City is nevertheless full of fine, full-flavoured patriotic fervour only shows that it is ready and eager to sink its interests in favour of those of its country.

Every knot that international finance ties between one country and another makes people in those two countries interested in their mutual good relations. The thing is so obvious, that, when one considers the number of these knots that have been tied since international finance first began to gather capital from one country's investors and place it at the disposal of others for the development of their resources, one can only marvel that the course of international goodwill has not made further progress. The fact that it is still a remarkably tender plant, likely to be crushed and withered by any breath of popular prejudice, is rather a comforting evidence of the slight importance that mankind attaches to the question of its bread and butter. It is clear that a purely material consideration, such as the interests of international finance, and the desire of those who have invested abroad to receive their dividends, weighs very little in the balance when the nations think that their honour or their national interests are at stake. Since the gilded cords of trade and finance have knit all the world into one great market, the proposition that war does not pay has become self-evident to any one who will give the question a few minutes' thought. International finance is a peacemaker every time it sends a British pound into a foreign country. But its influence as a peacemaker is astonishingly feeble just for this reason, that its appeal is to an interest which mankind very rightly disregards whenever it feels that more weighty matters are in question. The fact that war does not pay is an argument that is listened to as little by a nation when its blood is up, as the fact that being in love does not pay would be heeded by an amorous undergraduate.

If, then, the voice of international finance is so feeble when it is raised against the terrible scourge of war, can it have much force on the rare occasions when it speaks in its favour? For there is no inconsistency with the view that finance is a peacemaker, if we now acknowledge that finance may sometimes ask for the exertion of force on its behalf. As private citizens we all of us want to live at peace with our neighbours, but if one of them steals our property or makes a public nuisance of himself, we sometimes want to invoke the aid of the strong arm of the law in dealing with him. Consequently, although it cannot be true that finance wanted war such as this one, it cannot be denied that wars have happened in the past, which have been furthered by financiers who believed that they suffered wrongs which only war could put right. The Egyptian war of 1882 is a case in point, and the South African war of 1899 is another.

In Egypt international finance had lent money to a potentate ruling an economically backward people, without taking much trouble to consider how the money was to be spent, or whether the country could stand the charge on its revenues that the loans would involve. The fact that it did so was from one point of view a blunder and from another a crime, but this habit of committing blunders and crimes, which is sometimes indulged in by finance as by all other forms of human activity, will have to be dealt with in our next chapter, when we deal with the evils of international finance. The consequence of this blunder was that Egypt went into default, and England's might was used on behalf of the bondholders who had made a bad investment. This fact has been put forward by Mr. Brailsford, in his very interesting book on "The War of Steel and Gold," and by other writers, to show that our diplomacy is the tool of international finance, and that the forces created by British taxpayers for the defence of their country's honour, are used for the sordid purpose of wringing interest for a set of money-grubbers in the City, out of a poor and down-trodden peasantry overburdened by the exactions and extortions of their rulers. Mr. Brailsford, of course, puts his case much better than I can, in any brief summary of his views. He has earned and won the highest respect by his power as a brilliant writer, and by his disinterested and consistent championship of the cause of honesty and justice, wherever and whenever he thinks it to be in danger.

Nevertheless, in this matter of the Egyptian war I venture to think that he is mistaking the tail for the dog. Diplomacy, I fancy, was not wagged by finance, but used finance as a very opportune pretext. If Egypt had been Brazil, it is not very likely that the British fleet would have shelled Rio de Janeiro. The bondholders would have been reminded of the sound doctrine, *caveat emptor*, which signifies that those who make a bad bargain have only themselves to blame, and must pocket their loss with the best grace that they can muster. As it was, Egypt had long ago been marked out as a place that England wanted, because of its vitally important position on the way to India. Kinglake, the historian, writing some three-quarters of a century ago, long before the Suez Canal was built, prophesied that Egypt would some day be ours. In Chapter XX. of "Eothen," comes this well known passage on the Sphynx (he spelt it thus):—

> "And we, we shall die, and Islam will wither away, and the Englishman, leaning far over to hold his loved India, will plant a firm foot on the banks of the Nile, and sit in the seats of the Faithful, and still that sleepless rock will lie watching, and watching the works of the new, busy race, with those same sad, earnest eyes, and the same tranquil mien everlasting."

After the building of the Canal, the command of this short cut to India made Egypt still more important. England bought shares in the Canal, so using finance as a means to a political object; and it did so still more effectively when it used the Egyptian default and the claims of English bondholders as an excuse for taking its seat in Egypt and sitting there ever since. The bondholders were certainly benefited, but it is my belief that they might have whistled for their money until the crack of doom if it had not been that their claims chimed in with Imperial policy. It may have been wicked of us to take Egypt, but if so let us lay the blame on the right doorstep and not abuse the poor bondholder and financier who only wanted their money and were used as a stalking horse by the Machiavellis of Downing Street. Mr Brailsford's own account of the matter, indeed, shows very clearly that policy, and not finance, ruled the whole transaction.

In South Africa there was no question of default, or of suffering bondholders. There was a highly prosperous mining industry in a country that had formerly belonged to us, and had been given back to its Dutch inhabitants under circumstances which the majority of people in this country regarded as humiliating. On this occasion even the pretext was political. It may have been that the English mine-owners thought they could earn better profits under the British flag than under the rule of Mr. Kruger, though I am inclined to believe that even in their case their incentive was chiefly a patriotic desire to repaint in red that part of the map in which they carried on their business. Certainly their grievance, as it was put before us at home, was frankly and purely political. They said they wanted a vote and that Mr. Kruger would not give them one. That acute political thinker, Mr. Dooley of Chicago, pointed out at the time that if Mr. Kruger "had spint his life in a rale raypublic where they burn gas," he would have given them the votes, but done the counting himself. But Mr. Kruger did not adopt this cynical expedient, and public opinion here, though a considerable minority detested the war, endorsed the determination of the Government to restore the disputed British suzerainty over the Transvaal into actual sovereignty. Subsequent events, largely owing to the ample self-government given to the Transvaal immediately after its conquest, have shown that the war did more good than harm; and the splendid defeat of the Germans by the South African forces under General Botha—our most skilful opponent fifteen years ago—has, we may hope, wiped out all traces of the former conflict. But what we are now concerned with is the fact, which will be endorsed by all whose memory goes back to those days, that the South African war, though instigated and furthered by financial interests, would never have happened if public opinion had not been in favour of it on grounds which were quite other than financial—the desire to bring back the Transvaal into the British Empire and to wipe out the memory of the surrender after Majuba, and humanitarian feeling which believed, rightly or wrongly, that the natives would be treated better under our rule. These may or may not have been good reasons for going to war, but at least they were not financial.

Summing up the results of this rather discursive chapter we see that the chief benefit conferred on mankind by international finance is a quickening of the pace at which the wealth of the world is increased and multiplied, by using the capital saved by old countries for fostering the productive power of new ones. This is surely something solid on the credit side of the balance sheet, though it would be a good deal more so if mankind had made better progress with the much more difficult problem of using and distributing its wealth. If the rapid increase of wealth merely means that honest citizens, who find it as hard as ever to earn a living, are to be splashed with more mud from more motor-cars full of more road hogs, then there is little wonder if the results of international finance produce a feeling of disillusionment. But at least it must be admitted that the stuff has to be grown and made before it can be shared, and that a great advance has been made even in the general distribution of comfort. If we still find it hard to make a living, that is partly because we have very considerably expanded, during the course of the last generation or two, our notion of what we mean by a living.

As to the sinister influence alleged to be wielded by international finance in the councils of diplomacy, it has been shown that war on a great scale terrifies finance and inflicts great distress on it. To suppose, therefore, that finance is interested in the promotion of such wars is to suppose that it is a power shortsighted to the point of imbecility. In the case of wars which finance is believed with some truth to have helped to instigate, we have seen that it could not have done so if other influences had not helped it. In short, both the occurrence of the present war, and the circumstances that led up to war in Egypt and South Africa, have shown how little power finance wields in the realm of foreign politics. In the City if one suggests that our Foreign Office is swayed by financial influences one is met by incredulous mockery, probably accompanied by assertions that the Foreign Office is, in fact, neglectful, to a fault, of British financial interests abroad, and that when it does, as in China, interfere with financial matters, it is apt to tie the hands of finance, in order to further what it believes to be the political interests of the country. The formation of the Six Power Group in China meant that the financial strength of England and France had to be shared, for political reasons, with powers which had, on purely financial grounds, no claim whatever to participate in the business of furnishing capital to China. The introduction to the 1898 edition of "Fenn on the Funds," expresses the view that our Government is ready to protect our traders abroad, but only helps investors when it suits it to do so. "If," it says, "a barbarian potentate's subjects rob a British trader we never hesitate to insist upon the payment of liberal compensation, which we enforce if necessary by a 'punitive expedition,' but if a civilized Government robs a large number of British investors, the Government does not even, so far as we know, enlist the help of its diplomatic service. Only when, as in the case of Egypt, there are important political objects in view, does the State protect those citizens who are creditors of foreign nations. One or two other countries, notably Germany, set us a good example, with the best results as far as their investors are concerned." Germany is often thus taken as the example of the State which gives its financiers the most efficient backing abroad; but even in Germany finance is, like everything else, the obedient servant of the military and political authorities. For several years before the present war, the financiers of Berlin were forbidden to engage in moneylending operations abroad. No doubt the Government saw that the present war was coming, and so it preferred to keep German money at home. It is true that Germany once shook its mailed fist with some vigour on behalf of its financial interest when it made, with us, a demonstration against Venezuela. But it is at least possible that it did so chiefly with a view to the promotion of the popularity of its navy at home, and to making it easier to get the money for its upkeep and increase from the taxpayers, already oppressed by their military burden. In Morocco questions of trade and finance were at the back of the quarrel, but it would not have become acute if it had not been for the expected political consequences that were feared from the financial penetration that was being attempted; and as has been already pointed out, the financiers are generally credited with having persuaded Germany to agree to a settlement on that occasion.

In short, finance, if left to itself, is international and peace-loving. Many financiers are at the same time ardent patriots, and see in their efforts to enrich themselves and their own country a means for furthering its political greatness and diplomatic prestige. Man is a jumble of contradictory crotchets, and it would be difficult to find anywhere a financier who lived, as they are all commonly supposed to do, purely for the pleasure of amassing wealth. If such a being could be discovered he would probably be a lavish subscriber to peace societies, and would show a deep mistrust of diplomatists and politicians.

FOOTNOTES:

[4]

Quoted by the *Financial News* of September 28, 1915.

CHAPTER VI

THE EVILS OF INTERNATIONAL FINANCE

No one who writes of the evils of international finance runs any risk of being "gravelled for lack of matter." The theme is one that has been copiously developed, in a variety of keys by all sorts and conditions of composers. Since Philip the Second of Spain published his views on "financiering and unhallowed practices with bills of exchange," and illustrated them by repudiating his debts, there has been a chorus of opinion singing the same tune with variations, and describing the financier as a bloodsucker who makes nothing, and consumes an inordinate amount of the good things that are made by other people.

It has already been shown that capital, saved by thrifty folk, is essential to industry as society is at present built and worked; and the financiers are the people who see to the management of these savings, their collection into the great reservoir of the money market, and their placing at the disposal of industry. It seems, therefore, that, though not immediately concerned with the making of anything, the financiers actually do work which is now necessary to the making of almost everything. Railway managers do not make anything that can be touched or seen, but the power to move things from the place where they are grown or made, to the place where they are eaten or otherwise consumed or enjoyed, is so important that industry could not be carried on on its present scale without them; and that is only another way of saying that, if it had not been for the railway managers, a large number of us who at present do our best to enjoy life, could never have been born. Financiers are, if possible, even more necessary, to the present structure of industry than railway men. If, then, there is this general prejudice against people who turn an all important wheel in the machinery of modern production, it must either be based on some popular delusion, or if there is any truth behind it, it must be due to the fact that the financiers do their work ill, or charge the community too much for it, or both.

Before we can examine this interesting problem on its merits, we have to get over one nasty puddle that lies at the beginning of it. Much of the prejudice against financiers is based on, or connected with, anti-Semitic feeling, that miserable relic of medieval barbarism. No candid examination of the views current about finance and financiers can shirk the fact that the common prejudice against Jews is at the back of them; and the absurdity of this prejudice is a very fair measure of the validity of other current notions on the subject of financiers. The Jews are, chiefly, and in general, what they have been made by the alleged Christianity of the so-called Christians among whom they have dwelt. An obvious example of their treatment in the good old days, is given by Antonio's behaviour to Shylock. Antonio, of whom another character in the *Merchant of Venice* says that—

"A kinder gentleman treads not the earth,"

not only makes no attempt to deny that he has spat on the wicked Shylock, and called him cut-throat dog, but remarks that he is quite likely to do so again. Such was the behaviour towards Jews of the princely Venetian merchant, whom Shakespeare was portraying as a model of all the virtues.[5] Compare also, for a more modern example, Kinglake in a note to Chapter V of "Eothen."

> "The Jews of Smyrna are poor, and having little merchandize of their own to dispose of, they are sadly importunate in offering their services as intermediaries; their troublesome conduct had led to the custom of beating them in the open streets. It is usual for Europeans to carry long sticks with them, for the express purpose of keeping off the chosen people. I always felt ashamed to strike the poor fellows myself, but I confess to the amusement with which I witnessed the observance of this custom by other people."

Originally, as we see from the Hebrew scriptures, a hardy race of shepherds, farmers, and warriors, they were forced into the business of finance by the canonical law which forbade Christians to lend money at interest, and also by the persecution, robbery and risk of banishment to which Christian prejudice made them always liable. For these reasons they had to have their belongings in a form in which they could at any moment be concealed from robbers, or packed up and carried off if their owners suddenly found themselves told to quit their homes. So they were practically compelled to traffic in coins and precious metals and jewellery, and in many places all other trades and professions were expressly forbidden to them. This traffic in coins and metals naturally led to the business of moneylending and finance, and the centuries of practice, imposed on them by Christianity, have given them a skill in this trade, which is now the envy of Christians who have in the meantime found out that there is nothing wicked about moneylending, when it is honestly done. At the same time these centuries of persecution have given the Jews other qualities which we have more reason to envy than their skill in finance, such as their strong family affection and the steadfastness with which they stand by one another in all countries of the world. The fact of their being scattered over the face of the earth has given them added strength since finance became international. The great Jew houses have relations and connections in every business centre, and so their power has been welded, by centuries of racial prejudice, into a weapon the strength of which it is easy for popular imagination to exaggerate. Christendom forced the money power into the hands of this persecuted race, and now feels sorry when it sees that in an ordered and civilized society, in which it is no longer possible to roast an awkward creditor alive, money power is a formidable force. That a large part of this power is in the hands of a family party, scattered over all lands in which finance is possible, is another reason why, as I have already shown, international finance works for peace. The fact of the existence of the present war, however, shows that the limits of its power are soon reached, at times when the nations believe that their honour and safety can only be assured by bloodshed.

A large part of the popular prejudice against financiers may thus be ascribed to anti-Semitic feeling. We are still like the sailor who was found beating a Jew as a protest against the Crucifixion, and, when told that it had happened nearly two thousand years ago, said that he had only heard of it that morning.

But, when we have purged our minds of this stupid prejudice, we are still faced by the fact that international finance is often an unclean business, bad both for the borrower and for the lender and profitable only to a horde of parasites in the borrowing country, and to those who handle the loan in the lending country, and get subscriptions to it from investors who are subsequently sorry that they put their eggs into a basket with no bottom to it. Under ideal conditions our money is lent by us, through a first-rate and honourable finance house, to a country which makes honest use of it in developing its resources and increasing its power to make and grow things. The loan is taken out from England in the shape of goods and services required for the equipment of a young country, and the interest comes in every year in the shape of food and raw material that feeds us and helps our industry. Such, it may be asserted with confidence, is the usual course of events, and must have been so, or England could not have been so greatly enriched by her moneylending operations abroad, and the productive power of the world could not have grown as it has, under the top-dressing that our finance and trade have given it. But though it is thus clear enough that the business must have been on the whole honestly and soundly worked, there have been some ugly stains on its past, and its recent history has not been quite free from unsavoury features.

In 1875 public opinion was so deeply stirred by the manner in which English investors and borrowing states had suffered from the system by which the business of international finance was handled, that a Select Committee of the House of Commons was "appointed to inquire into the circumstances attending the making of contracts for Loans with certain Foreign States and also the causes which have led to the non-payment of the principal moneys and interest due in respect of such loans." Its report is a very interesting document, well worth the attention of those interested in the vagaries of human folly. It will astound the reader by reason of the wickedness of the waste of good capital involved, and at the same time it is a very pleasant proof of the progress that has been made in finance during the last half century. It is almost incredible that such things should have happened so lately. It is quite impossible that they could happen now.

In 1867 the Republic of Honduras had been for forty years in default on its portion, amounting to £27,200, of a loan issued in London in 1825, for the Federal States of Central America. Nevertheless it contracted with Messrs. B---- and G---- for a loan of £1,000,000 to be issued in Paris and London. The loan was to be secured on a railway, to be built, or begun, out of its proceeds, and by a first mortgage on all the domains and forests of the State. The Government undertook to pay £140,000 annually for fifteen years, to meet interest on and redemption of the loan. As it had been forty years in default on a loan which only involved a charge of £1632, it is hard to imagine how the State could have entered into such a liability, or how any issuing house could have had the temerity to put it before the public.

The public was the only party to the proceedings which showed any sense. Don C---- G----, representative of the Honduras Government in London, relates in the record of these events that he put before the Committee, that "the First Honduras Loan in spite of all the advantages which it offered to subscribers" [issue price, 80, interest 10 per cent., sinking fund of 3 per cent, which would redeem the whole loan at par within 17 years] "and the high respectability of the house which managed the operation, was received by the public with perfect indifference, with profound contempt; and according to the deficient and vague information which reached the Legation, there were hardly any other subscriptions than one of about £10,000 made by the firm of B----itself," Don G----, however, seems to have slightly exaggerated the wisdom of the public; in any case the Committee found that by June 30, 1868, by some means £48,000 of the loan was held by the public, and £952,000 was in possession of the representatives of the Honduras Government. On that day a Mr. L---- undertook to take over the Government's holding at £68 12s. per bond, and pay current interest. A market was made, brokers were prevailed on to interest their friends in the security, and in two years' time the bonds were disposed of. The quotation was skilfully kept above the issue price and in November, 1868, it reached 94.

The story of this loan is complicated by the fact that half of it was at the time alleged to have been placed in Paris, but it appears, as far as one can disentangle fact from the twisted skein of the report, that the Paris placing must have resulted much as did the first effort made in London, and that practically the whole of the bonds there issued came back into the hands of the representatives of Honduras.

At the end of the proceedings the whole amount of the loan seemed to have been disposed of in London, £631,000 having been sold to Mr. L---- and passed on by him by the means described above, £200,000 having been issued to railway contractors, £10,800 having been "drawn before issue and cancelled," while £49,500 was "issued in exchange for scrip," and £108,500 was taken on account of commission and expenses.

The actual cash received on account of this loan appears, though the Committee's figures are difficult to follow, to have come to just over half a million. Out of the half million £16,850 went in cash commission, and £106,000 in interest and sinking fund, leaving about £380,000 for the railway contractors and the Government. On this loan the Committee observes that the commission paid, of £108,500 bonds, and £16,850 in cash was "greatly in excess of what is usually charged by contractors for loans."

So far it was only a case of a thoroughly speculative transaction carried through by means of the usual accompaniments. A defaulting State believed to be possessed of great potential wealth, thought, or was induced to think, that by building a railway it could tap that wealth. The whole thing was a pure possibility. If the loan had been successfully placed at the issue price it would have sufficed to build the first section (fifty-three miles) of railway, and to leave something over for work in the mahogany forests. It is barely possible that in time the railway might have enabled the Government to produce enough stuff out of its forests to meet the charges of the loan. But the possibility was so remote that the terms offered had to be so liberal that they frightened the public, which happened to be in a sensible mood, until it was induced to buy by the creation of a market on the Stock Exchange; the employment of intermediaries on disastrous terms, and finally default, as soon as the loan charge could no longer be paid out of the proceeds of the loan, completed the tale.

In May, 1869, the Minister for Honduras in Paris, M. H----, "took steps" to issue a loan for 62,250,060 francs, or £2,490,000. Out of it a small sum (about £62,000) was paid to the railway contractors in London, but little of it seems to have been genuinely placed, since, when the Franco-German war broke out in July, 1870, M. H---- sent 2,500,000 francs in cash (£100,000), and 39,000,000 francs in bonds, to Messrs. B---- and G---- in London. Messrs. B---- and others made an agreement with Mr. C. L----, presumably the gentleman who had taken over and dealt with the unplaced balance of the First London Loan. By its terms the net price to be paid by him for each 300 francs (£12) bond issued originally at 225 francs (£9), was 124 francs (not quite £5). He succeeded in selling bonds enough to realize £408,460, and he, together with Messrs. B---- and G----, received £51,852 in commission for so doing.

In the spring of 1870, the Honduras Government, still hankering after its railway and the wealth that it was to open up, determined to try again with another loan. Something had to be done to encourage investors to take it. A few days before the prospectus appeared a statement was published in a London newspaper to the effect that two ships had arrived in the West India Docks from Truxillo (Honduras) with cargoes of mahogany and fustic consigned to Messrs. B---- and G----on account of the Honduras Railway Loan, and that two others were loading at Truxillo with similar cargoes on the same account. These cargoes had not been cut by the Honduras Government. It had bought them from timber merchants, and they were found to be of most inferior quality. In the opinion of the Committee "the purchase of these cargoes and the announcement of their arrival in the form above referred to, were intended to induce, and did induce, the public to believe that the hypothecated forests were providing means for paying the interest upon the loan."

With the help of this fraud, and with a free and extensive market made on the Stock Exchange, the 1870 Honduras 10 per cent. loan for £2,500,000 nominal was successfully issued at 80. It also had a sinking fund of 3 per cent., which was to pay it off in fifteen years. Mr. L---- again handled the operation, having taken over the contract from Messrs. B---- and G----. But the success of the issue was more than hollow. It was empty. For Mr. L----, in the process of making the market to promote it, had bought nearly the whole loan. Applicants had evidently sold nearly as fast as they applied; for on the 15th December, when the last instalment was to be paid, less than £200,000 bonds remained in the hands of the public. Nevertheless by October, 1872, nearly the whole of the loan had been somehow disposed of to investors or speculators. One of the means taken to stimulate the demand for them was the announcement of extra drawings of bonds at par, over and above the operation of the 3 per cent, sinking fund, provided by the prospectus.

There is no need to linger over the complicated details of this sordid story. The Committee's report sums up, as follows, the net results of the 1869 and 1870 loans of Honduras:—

"In tracing the disposal of the proceeds of the 1869 and 1870 loans, it must be remembered that your Committee had no evidence before them relating to the funds resulting from three-fifths of the loan of 1869; only two-fifths of the loan was realized in this country, the remainder was disposed of in Paris before August, 1870, and no account of the application of the funds resulting from such portion of the loan could be obtained.

"The two-fifths of the 1869 loan, and the whole of the loan of 1870, produced net £2,051,511; out of this sum only £145,254 has been paid to the railway contractors; a sum of £923,184 would have been sufficient to discharge the interest and sinking fund in respect of the issued bonds of the three loans, yet the trustees ... paid to Mr. L----£1,339,752 or £416,568 beyond the sum so required to be paid upon the issued bonds of the loans.

"There was paid to him for commissions (apart from expenses) on the three loans, out of the above proceeds, the sum of £216,852. He also received out of the same proceeds £41,090, being the difference between £370,000 cash paid to him by the trustees and £328,910 scrip returned by him to them. This £41,090 probably represents the premiums paid on the purchase of the scrip before or immediately after the allotment of the loan, and was certainly a misapplication of the proceeds of the loan.

"Mr. L---- was also paid, out of these proceeds, a further sum of £57,318, nearly the whole of which seems to be a payment in discharge of an allowance of £8 per bond in respect of the dealings in the 1867 loan.... In addition ... it will be remembered that Mr. L---- received £50,000 'to maintain the credit of Honduras.'

"He also on the 18th of June, 1872, obtained £173,570 by delivering to the trustees ... 5042 bonds of the 1870 loan, at £75 Per bond and 33,000 bonds of the 1869 loan at 104 francs per bond, and retaking them at the same time from the trustees at £50 and 104 francs per bond respectively. Mr. L---- had contracted to pay for these bonds and they had been issued to him at the prices of £75 and 104 francs respectively, and the remission in the price therefore amounted to a gift to him of £173,570 ... out of this portion of the loan of 1869, and the loan of 1870, Mr. L----has received in cash, or by the remission of his contracts, £955,398."

It is little wonder that Honduras has been in default on these loans ever since. In its Report the Committee commented severely on the action of Don C----- G----, the London representative of the Republic. "He sanctioned," it says, "Stock Exchange dealings and speculations in the loans which no Minister should have sanctioned. He was a party to the purchase of the mahogany cargoes, and permitted the public to be misled by the announcements in relation to them. By express contract he authorized the 'additional drawings.' He assisted Mr. L---- to appropriate to himself large sums out of the proceeds of the loans to which he was not entitled." Very likely he had not a notion as to what the whole thing meant, and only thought that he was doing his best to finance his country along the road to wealth. But the fact remains that by these actions he made his Government a party to the proceedings that were so unfortunate for it and so ruinous to the holders of its bonds.

After its examination of these and other less sensational but equally disastrous issues the Committee made various recommendations, chiefly in the direction of greater publicity in prospectuses, and ended by expressing their conviction that "the best security against the recurrence of such evils as they have above described will be found, not so much in legislative enactments, as in the enlightenment of the public as to their real nature and origin."

If the scandals and losses involved by loan issues were always on this Gargantuan scale, there would be little difficulty about disposing of them, both on economic and moral grounds, and showing that there is, and can be, only one side to the problem. But when it is only a question, not of fraud on a great scale but of a certain amount of underhand business, such as is quite usual in some latitudes, and a certain amount of doubt as to the use that is likely to be made by the borrower of the money placed at its disposal, it is not so easy to feel sure about the duty of an issuing house in handling foreign loans. At a point, in fact, the question becomes full of subtleties and casuistical difficulties.

For instance, let us suppose that an emissary of the Republic of Barataria approaches a London issuing house and intimates that it wants a loan for 3 millions sterling, to be spent half in increasing the Republic's navy, and half in covering a deficit in its Budget, and that he, the said emissary, has full power to treat for the loan, and that a commission of 2 per cent. is to be paid to him by the issuing house, which can have the loan at a price that will easily enable it to pay this commission. That is to say, we will suppose that the Republic will take 85 for the price of its bonds, which are to carry 5 per cent. interest, to be secured by a lien on the customs receipts, and to be redeemed in thirty years' time by a cumulative Sinking Fund working by annual drawings at par, or by purchase in the market if the bonds can be bought below par. If the Republic's existing 5 per cent. bonds stand, let us say, at 98 in the market, this gives the issuing house a good prospect of being able to sell the new ones easily at 95, and so it has a 10 per cent. margin out of which to pay stamps, underwriting and other expenses, and commission to the intermediary who brought the proposal, and to keep a big profit to themselves. From the point of view of their own immediate interest there is every reason why they should close with the bargain, especially if we assume that the Republic is fairly rich and prosperous, and that there is little fear that its creditors will be left in the lurch by default.

From the point of view of national interest there is also much to be said for concluding the transaction. We may, with very good ground, assume that it would also be intimated to the issuing house that a group of Continental financiers was very willing to take the business up, that it had only been offered to it owing to old standing relations between it and the Republic, and that, if it did not wish to do the business, the loan would readily be raised in Paris or Berlin. By refusing, the London firm would thus prevent all the profit made by the operation from coming to England instead of to a foreign centre. But there is much more behind. For we have seen that finance and trade go hand-in-hand, and that when loan-houses in the City make advances to foreign countries, the hives of industry in the North are likely to be busy. It has not been usual here to make any express stipulation to the effect that the money, or part of it, raised by a loan is to be spent in England, but it is clear that when a nation borrows in England it is thereby predisposed to giving orders to English industry for goods that it proposes to buy. And even if it does not do so, the mere fact that England promises, by making the loan, to hand over so much money, in effect obliges her to sell goods or services valued at that amount as was shown on an earlier page.[6] On the Continent, this stipulation is usual. So that the issuing house would know that, if they make the loan, it is likely that English shipbuilders will get the orders on which part of it is to be spent, and that in any case English industry in one form or another will be drawn on to supply goods or services to somebody; whereas if they refuse the business it is certain that the industrial work involved will be lost to England.

On the other side of the account there are plenty of good reasons against the business. In the first place the terms offered are so onerous to the borrower that it may safely be said that no respectable issuing house in London would look at them. In effect the Republic would be paying nearly 6 per cent, on the money, if it sold its 5 per cent. bonds at 85, and the state of its credit, as expressed by the price of its bonds in the market, would not justify such a rate. The profit offered to the issuing house is too big, and the commission demanded by the intermediary is so large that it plainly points to evil practices in Barataria. It means that interested parties have made underhand arrangements with the Finance Minister, and that the Republic is going to be plundered, not in the fine full-flavoured style that ruled in earlier generations, but to an extent that makes the business too disreputable to handle. Any honourable English house would consider that the terms offered to itself and the conditions proposed by the emissary were such that the operation was suspicious, and that being mixed up with suspicious business was a luxury that it preferred to leave alone.

On other grounds the loan, well secured as it seems to be, is not of a kind to be encouraged. We have supposed its purpose to be, firstly, to meet a deficit in a Budget, and secondly, to pay for naval expansion. Neither of these objects is going to improve the financial position of the Republic. Covering a deficit by loan is bad finance in any case, but especially so when the loan is raised abroad. In the latter case it is most likely that the borrowing State is outrunning the constable, by importing more goods than it can pay for out of current production.

If it imports for the purpose of increasing its productive power by buying such things as railway material, then it is making a perfectly legitimate use of its credit, as long as the money is well spent, and the railways are honestly built, with a prospect of opening up good country, and are not put into the wrong place for political or other reasons. But if this were so, the money would not be wanted to balance a Budget, but on railway capital account. When a balance has to be filled by borrowing it can only mean that the State has spent more than its revenue from taxes permits, and that it is afraid to cut down its expenses by retrenchment or to increase its revenue by taxing more highly. And so it chooses the primrose path of dalliance with a moneylender.

As to naval expenditure, here again we have bad finance writ large over the proposal. It is not good business for countries to borrow in order to increase their armies and navies in time of peace, and the practice is especially objectionable when the loan is raised abroad. In time of war, when expenditure has to be so great and so rapid, that the taxpayers could not be expected to have it all taken out of their pockets by the tax-gatherer, there is some excuse for borrowing for naval and military needs; though even in time of war, if we could imagine an ideal State, with every citizen truly patriotic, and properly educated in economics and finance, and with wealth so fairly distributed and taxation so fairly imposed that there would be no possibility of any feeling of grievance and irritation among any class of taxpayers, it would probably decide that the simplest and most honest way of financing war is to do so wholly out of taxation. In time of peace, borrowing for expenditure on defence simply means that the cost of a need of to-day is met by someone who is hired to meet it, by a promise of interest and repayment, the provision of which is passed on to the citizens of to-morrow. It is always urged, of course, that the citizens of to-morrow are as deeply interested in the defence of the realm that they are to inherit as those of to-day, but that argument ignores the obvious fact that to-morrow will bring its own problems of defence with it, which seem likely to be at least as costly as those of the present day. Another objection to lending economically backward countries money to be invested in ships, is that we thereby encourage them to engage in shipbuilding rivalry, and to join in that race for aggressive power which has laid so sore a burden on the older peoples. The business is also complicated by the unpleasant activities of the armament firms of all countries, which are said to expend much ingenuity in inducing the Governments of the backward peoples to indulge in the luxury of battleships. Here, again, there is no need to paint too lurid a picture. The armament firms are manufacturers with an article to sell, which is important to the existence of any nation with a seaboard; and they are entirely justified in legitimate endeavours to push their wares. The fact that the armament firms of England, Germany, and France had certain interests in common, is often used as a text for sermons on the subject of the unpatriotic cynicism of international finance. It is easy to paint them as a ring of cold-blooded devils trying to stimulate bloodthirsty feeling between the nations so that there may be a good market for weapons of destruction. From their point of view, they are providers of engines of defence which they make, in the first place, for the use of their own country, and are ready to supply also, in time of peace, to other nations in order that their plant may be kept running, and the cost of production may be kept low. This is one of the matters on which public opinion may have something to say when the war is over. In the meantime it may be noted that unsavoury scandals have occasionally arisen in connection with the placing of battleship orders, and that this is another reason why a loan to finance them is likely to have an unpleasant flavour in the nostrils of the fastidious.

But if we admit the very worst that the most searching critic of international finance can allege against the proposal that we imagine to be put forward by the Republic of Barataria—if we admit that a loan to balance a deficit and pay for ships probably implies wastefulness, corruption, political rottenness, impecunious Chauvinism and all the rest of it, the question still arises whether it is the business of an issuing house to refuse the chance of doing good business for itself and for the London money-market, because it has reason to believe that the money lent will not be well spent. In the case supposed, we have seen that the terms offered and the commission to be made by the intermediary were such that the latter would have been shown the door. But if these matters had been satisfactory, ought the proposal to have been rejected because the loan was to be raised for unproductive purposes?

In other words, is it the business of an issuing house to take care of the economic morals of its clients, or is it merely concerned to see that the securities which it offers to the public are well secured? In ordinary life, and in the relations between moneylender and borrower at home, no such question could be asked. If I went to my banker and asked for a loan and gave him security that he thought good enough, it would not occur to him to ask what I was going to do with the money—whether I was going to use it in a way that would increase my earning capacity, or on building myself a billiard room and a conservatory, or on a visit to Monte Carlo. He would only be concerned with making sure that any of his depositors' money that he lent to me would be repaid in due course, and the manner in which I used or abused the funds lent to me would be a question in which I only was concerned. If it is the business of an international finance house to be more careful about the use to which money that it lends on behalf of clients is put, why should this be so?

There are several reasons. First, because if the borrower does not see fit to pay interest on the loan or repay it when it falls due, there is no process of law by which the lender can recover. If I borrow from my banker and then default on my debt, he can put me in the bankruptcy court, and sell me up. Probably he will have protected himself by making me pledge securities that he can seize if I do not pay, a safeguard which cannot be had in the case of international borrowing; but if these securities are found to be of too little value to make the debt good, everything else that I own can be attached by him. The international moneylender, on the other hand, if his debtor defaults may, if he is lucky, induce his Government to bring diplomatic pressure to bear, for whatever that may be worth. If there is a political purpose to be served, as in Egypt, he may even find himself used as an excuse for armed intervention, in the course of which his claims will be supported, and made good. In many cases, however, he and the bondholders who subscribed to his issue simply have to say goodbye to their money, with the best grace that they can muster, in the absence of any law by which a lender can recover moneys advanced to a sovereign State. With this essential difference in the conditions under which a banker lends his depositors' money to a local customer, and those under which an international house lends its clients' money to a borrowing country, it follows that the responsible party in the latter case ought to exercise very much more care to see that the money is well spent.

In the second place, the customers to whom bankers, in economically civilized lands, lend the money entrusted to them, may fairly be presumed to know something about the use and abuse of money and to be able to take care of themselves. If they borrow money, and then waste it or spend it in riotous living, they know that they will presently impoverish themselves, and that they will be the sufferers. But in the case of a young country, with all its financial experience yet unbought, there is little or no reason for supposing that its rulers are aware that they cannot eat their cake and have it. They probably think that by borrowing to meet a deficit or to build a Dreadnought they are doing something quite clever, dipping their hands into a horn of plenty that a kindly Providence has designed for their behoof, and that the loan will somehow, some day, get itself paid without any trouble to anybody. Moreover, if they are troubled with any forebodings, the voice of common sense is likely to be hushed by the reflection that they personally will not be the sufferers, but the great body of taxpayers, or in the case of actual default, the deluded bondholders; and that in any case, the trouble caused by over-borrowing and bad spending is not likely to come to a head for some years. Its first effect is a flush of fictitious prosperity which makes everybody happy and enhances the reputation of the ministers who have arranged it. When, years after, the evil seed sown has brought to light its crops of tares, it is very unlikely that the chain of cause and effect will be recognized by its victims, who are much more likely to lay the bad harvest to the door not of the bad financier who sowed it, but of some innocent and perhaps wholly virtuous successor, merely because it was during his term of office that the crop was garnered. So many are the inducements offered to young States, with ignorant or evil (or both) rulers at their head, to abuse the facilities given them by international finance, that there is all the more reason why those who hold the strings of its purse should exercise very great caution in allowing them to dip into it.

There is yet another reason why the attitude of an issuing house, to a borrowing State, should be paternal or even grand-motherly, as compared with the purely business-like attitude of a banker to a local borrower. If the bank makes a bad debt, it has to make it good to its depositors at the expense of its shareholders. It diminishes the amount that can be paid in dividends and so the bank is actually out of pocket. The international financier is in quite a different position. If he arranges a loan for Barataria, he takes his profit on the transaction, sells the bonds to investors, or to the underwriters if investors do not apply, and is, from the purely business point of view, quit of the whole operation. He still remains responsible for receiving from the State, and paying to the bondholders, the sum due each half year in interest, and for seeing to the redemption of the bonds by the operation of the Sinking Fund, if any. But if anything goes wrong with the interest or Sinking Fund he is not liable to the bondholders, as the bank is liable to its depositors. They have got their bonds, and if the bonds are in default they have made a bad debt and not the issuing house, unless, as is unlikely, it has kept any of them in its own hands.

But this absence of any legal liability on the part of the issuing house imposes on it a very strong moral obligation, which is fully recognized by the best of them. Just because the bondholders have no right of action against it, unless it can be shown that it issued a prospectus containing incorrect statements, it is all the more bound to see that their money shall not be imperilled by any action of its own. It knows that a firm with a good reputation as an international finance house has only to put its name to an issue, and a large number of investors, who have neither the education nor the knowledge required to form a judgment on its merits, will send in subscriptions for the bonds on the strength of the name of the issuing house. This fact makes it an obvious duty on the part of the latter to see that this trust is deserved. Moreover, it would obviously be bad business on their part to neglect this duty. For a good reputation as an issuing house takes years to build up, and is very easily shaken by any mistake, or even by any accident, which could not have been foreseen but yet brings a loan that it has handled into the list of doubtful payers. Mr. Brailsford, indeed, asserts that it may be to the advantage of bondholders to be faced by default on the part of their debtors. It may be so in those rare cases in which they can get reparation and increased security, as in the case of our seizure of Egypt. But in nine cases out of ten, as is shown by the plaintive story told by the yearly reports of the Council of

Foreign Bondholders, default means loss and a shock to confidence, even if only temporary, and is generally followed by a composition involving a permanent reduction in debt and interest. Investors who have suffered these unpleasantnesses are likely to remember them for many a long year, and to remember also the name of the issuing house which fathered the loan that was the cause of the trouble.

There are thus many good reasons why it is the business of a careful issuing firm to see not only that any loan that it offers is well secured, but also that it is to be spent on objects that will not impair the productive capacity of the borrowing country by leading it down the path of extravagance, but will improve it by developing its resources or increasing its power to move its products. On the other hand, the temptation to undertake bad business on behalf of an importunate borrower is great. The profits are considerable for the issuing house and for all their followers in the City. The indirect advantages, in the way of trade orders, conferred on the lending country, are also profitable, and there is always the fear that if London firms take too austere a view of what is good business for them and the borrowing countries, the more accommodating loan-mongers of foreign centres may reap the benefit, and leave them with empty pockets and the somewhat chilly comfort conferred by the consciousness of a high ideal in finance.

One of the most unsatisfactory features about the monetary arrangements of society, as at present constituted, is the fact that the reward of effort is so often greater with every degree of evil involved by the effort. And to some extent this is true in finance. Just as big fortunes are made by the cheap-jacks who stuff the stomachs of an ignorant public with patent medicines, while doctors slave patiently for a pittance on the unsavoury task of keeping overfed people in health; just as Milton got £5 for "Paradise Lost," while certain modern novelists are rewarded with thousands of pounds for writing romances which would never be printed in a really educated community; so in finance the more questionable—up to a certain point—be the security to be handled, the greater are the profits of the issuing house, the larger the commissions of the underwriters and brokers, and the larger are the amounts paid to the newspapers for advertising. As has already been observed, that part of the City that lives on handling new issues has been half starved since the war began, because its activities have been practically confined to loans issued by the British Government. These loans have been huge in amount but there has been no underwriting, and brokerages are cut to the bone. Advertising for the second War Loan was on a great scale, but in proportion to the amount subscribed the cost of it was probably small, according to the ideals that ruled before the war. A Colonial loan, or a first-class American railroad bond, almost places itself, and the profits on the issue to all who handle it are proportionately low. The more questionable the security, the more it has to pay for its footing, and the higher are the profits of those who father it and assist the process of delivery, as long, that is, as the birth is successfully accomplished.

If there is failure, partial or complete, then the task of holding the baby is longer and more uncomfortable, the more puny and unattractive it is. If, owing to some accident in the monetary atmosphere, a Colonial loan does not go off well, the underwriters who find themselves saddled with it, can easily borrow on it, in normal times, and know that sooner or later trustees and other real investors will take it off their hands. But if it is an issue of some minor European power, or of some not too opulent South American State, that is coldly received by the investing public, bankers will want a big margin before they accept it as security for an advance, and it may take years to find a home for it in the strong boxes of real investors, and then perhaps only at a price that will leave the underwriters, like Sir Andrew Aguecheek, "a foul way out." There is thus a logical reason for the higher profits attached to the more questionable issues, and this reason is found in the greater risk attached, if failure should ensue.

Thus we arrive at the reply to those who criticize International Finance on the ground that it puts too big profits into the pockets of those who handle it. If the profits are big, it is only in the case of loan issues which carry with them a considerable risk to the reputation of the fathering firm, and to the pockets of the underwriters, and involve a responsibility, and in the case of default, an amount of wholly unpaid work and anxiety for which the big profits made on the opening proceedings do not nearly compensate. As in the case of the big gains made by patent pill merchants, and bad novelists, it is the public, which is so fond of grumbling because other people make fortunes out of it, that is really responsible for their doing so, by reason of its own greed and stupidity. Because it will not take the trouble to find out how to spend or invest its money, it asks those who are clever enough to batten on its foibles, to sell it bad stuff and bad securities, and then feels hurt because it has a pain in its inside, or a worthless bond at its banker's, while the producers thereof are founding county families. If the public would learn the A B C of investment, and also learn that there is an essential difference between investment and speculation, that they will not blend easily but are likely to spoil one another if one tries to mix them, then the whole business of loan issuing and company promotion would be on a sounder basis, with less risk to those who handle it, and less temptation to them to try for big profits out of bad ventures. But as long as

"the fool multitude that choose by show"

give more attention to the size of an advertisement than to the merits of the security that it offers, the profits of those who cater for its weaknesses will wax fat.

When all has been said that can be urged against the record of international finance, the fact remains that from the purely material point of view it has done a great work in increasing the wealth of mankind. It is true that capital has often been wasted by being lent to corrupt or improvident borrowers for purposes which were either objectionable in themselves, or which ought to have been financed, if at all, out of current revenue. It is true, also, that crimes have been committed, as in the case of the Putumayo horrors, when the money of English shareholders has been invested in the exploitation of helpless natives, accompanied by circumstances of atrocious barbarity. Nevertheless if we compare the record of finance with that of religion or international politics, it stands out as by far the cleanest of the influences that have worked upon the mutual relations of the various groups of mankind. International Finance makes a series of bargains between one nation and another, for the mutual benefit of each, complicated by occasional blunders, some robbery, and, in exceptional cases, horrible brutality. Religion has stained history with the most ruthless massacres, and the most unspeakable ingenuity in torture, all devised for the glory of God, and the furtherance of what its devotees believed to be His word. International politics have plunged mankind into a series of bloody and destructive wars, culminating in the present cataclysm. Finance can only prosper through production; its efforts are inevitably failures, if they do not tend to the growing and making of things, or the production of services, that are wanted. Destruction, reduced to a fine art and embellished by the nicest ingenuities of the most carefully applied science, is the weapon of international politics.

> *Note.*—The names of the actors in the Honduras drama were printed in blank because it seemed unfair to do otherwise, in revising fifty years' old scandals, as an example of what International Finance can do at its worst.

FOOTNOTES:

[5]

Merchant of Venice, I, 3.

[6]

Pages 75, 76.

CHAPTER VII

NATIONALISM AND FINANCE

So far we have considered the working of International Finance chiefly from the point of view of its effects upon the prosperity and comfort of mankind as a whole and on this country, as the greatest trader, carrier, and financier of the world. We have seen that the benefit that it works is wrought chiefly through specialization, that is, through the production of the good things of the earth in the lands best fitted, by climate or otherwise, to grow and make them. By lending money to other lands, and the goods and service that they have bought with it, we have helped them to produce things for us to consume, or to work up into other things for our consumption or that of other peoples. Thereby we have enriched ourselves and the rest of mankind. But the question still arises whether this process is one that should be left altogether unchecked, or whether it involves evils which go far to modify its benefits. In other words is it a good thing for us, socially and politically, to enrich ourselves beyond a certain point by a process which involves our dependence on other countries for food and raw material?

Analogy between a State and a man is often useful, if not pushed too far. The original man in a primitive state is always assumed to have been bound to find or make everything that he wanted by his own exertions. He was hut builder, hunter, cultivator, bow-maker, arrow-maker, trapper, fisherman, boat-builder, leather-dresser, tailor, fighter—a wonderfully versatile and self-sufficient person. As the process grew up of specialization, and the exchange of goods and services, all the things that were needed by man were made much better and more cheaply, but this was only brought about at the expense of each man's versatility. Nowadays we can all of us do something very much better than the primitive savage, but we cannot do everything nearly as well. We have become little insignificant wheels in a mighty great machine that feeds us and clothes us and provides us with comforts and luxuries of which he could never have dreamt. He was the whole of his machine, and was thereby a far more completely developed man. The modern millionaire, in spite of his enormous indirect power over the forces of nature, is a puny and ineffective being by the side of his savage ancestor, in the matter of power to take care of himself with his own hands and feet and eyes, and with weapons made by his own ingenuity and cunning. Moreover, though in the case of the millionaire and of all the comparatively well-to-do classes we can point to great intellectual and artistic advantages, and many pleasant amenities of life now enjoyed by them, thanks to the process of specialization, these advantages can only be enjoyed to the full by comparatively few. To the majority specialization has brought a life of mechanical and monotonous toil, with little or none of the pride in a job well done, such as was enjoyed by the savage when he had made his bow or caught his fish; those who work all day on some minute process necessary, among many others, to the turning out of a pin, can never feel the full joy of achievement such as is gained by a man who has made the whole of anything. Pins are made much faster, but some of the men who make them remain machines, and never become men at all in the real sense of the word. And when at the same time the circumstances of their lives, apart from their work, are all that they should not be—bad food, bad clothes, bad education, bad houses, foul atmosphere and dingy and sordid surroundings, it is very obvious that to a large part of working mankind, the benefits of the much vaunted division of labour have been accompanied by very serious drawbacks. The best that can be said is that if it had not been for the division of labour a large number of them could never have come into existence at all; and the question remains whether any sort of existence is better than none.

In the case of a nation the process of specialization has not, for obvious reasons, gone nearly so far. Every country does a certain amount of farming and of seafaring (if it has a seaboard), and of manufacturing. But the tendency has been towards increasing specialization, and the last results of specialization, if carried to its logical end, are not nice to forecast. "It is not pleasant," wrote a distinguished statistician, "to contemplate England as one vast factory, an enlarged Manchester, manufacturing in semi-darkness, continual uproar and at an intense pressure for the rest of the world. Nor would the continent of America, divided into square, numbered fields, and cultivated from a central station by electricity, be an ennobling spectacle."[1]

It need not be said that the horrible consequences of specialization depicted by Dr. Bowley need not necessarily have happened, even if its effects has been given free play. But the interesting point about his picture, at the present moment, is the fact that it was drawn from the purely economic and social point of view. He questioned whether it was really to the advantage of a nation, regarding only its own comfort and well-being, to allow specialization to go beyond a certain point. It had already arrived at a point at which land was going out of cultivation in England, and was being more and more regarded as a park, pleasure ground and sporting place for people who made, or whose forbears had made, fortunes out of commerce and finance, and less and less as a means for supplying food for our workers, and raw material for our industries. The country workers were going to the new countries that our capital was opening up, or into the towns to learn industrial crafts, or taking services as gamekeepers, grooms or chauffeurs, with the well-to-do classes who earned their profits from industry or business. Even before the war there was a growing scarcity of labour to grow, and harvest, even the lessened volume of our agricultural output. Dr. Bowley's picture was far from being realized and even if the process of specialization had gone on, it may be hoped that we should have had sense enough to avoid the blackest of its horrors.

Then came the war, which went far to undermine the great underlying assumption on which the free interchange of capital among nations and the consequent specialization that proceeded from it, was taken to be a safe and sound policy. This assumption was in effect, that the world was civilized to a point at which there was no need to fear that its whole economic arrangements would be upset by war. We now know that the world was not civilized to this point, and is a very long way from being so, that the ultimate appeal is still to "arms and the man," and that we have still to be careful to see that our trade and industry are carried on in such a way as to be least likely to be hurt if ploughshares have suddenly to be beaten into swords. At first sight, this is a somewhat tragical discovery, but it carries with it certain consolations. If the apparent civilization evolved by the nineteenth century had been good and wholesome, it might have been really sad to find that it was only a thin veneer laid over a structure that man's primitive passions might at any moment overturn. In fact, the apparently achieved civilization was so grossly material in its successes, so forcibly feeble in its failures, so beset with vulgarity at its summit and undermined by destitution at its base, that even the horrors of the present war, with its appalling loss of the best lives of the chief nations of the earth, may be a blessing to mankind in the long run if they purge its notions about the things that are worth trying for.

At least the war is teaching us that the wealth of a nation is not a pile of commodities to be frittered away in vulgar ostentation and stupid self-indulgence, but the number of its citizens who are able and ready to play the man as workers or fighters when a time of trial comes. "National prosperity," says Cobbett, "shows itself ... in the plentiful meal, the comfortable dwelling, the decent furniture and dress, the healthy and happy countenances, and the good morals of the labouring classes of the people." So he wrote, in Newgate gaol, in 1810.[8] Since then many reformers have preached the same sound doctrine, but its application has made poor progress, in relation to the growth of our riches in the same period. If we now decide to put it into practice, we shall not long tolerate the existence in our midst of disease and destitution, and a system of distribution of the world's goods which gives millions of our population no chance of full development.

We need not, then, stay to shed tears over the civilization, such as it was, which we thought we had and had not. Its good points will endure, for evil has a comfortable habit of killing itself and those who work it. All that we are concerned with at this moment is the fact that its downfall has shaken an article in our economic faith which taught us that specialization was a cause of so much more good than evil, that its development by the free spreading of our capital all over the world, wherever the demand for it gave most profit to the owner, was a tendency to be encouraged, or at least to be left free to work out its will. This was true enough to be a platitude as long as we could rely on peace. Our capital went forth and fertilized the world, and out of its growing produce the world enriched us. As the world developed its productive power, its goods poured into us, as the great free mart where all men were welcome to sell their wares. These goods came in exchange for our goods and services, and the more we bought the more we sold. When other nations took to dealing direct with one another, they wanted our capital to finance the business, and our ships to carry the goods. The world as a whole could not grow in wealth without enriching the people that was the greatest buyer and seller, the greatest moneylender and the greatest carrier. It was all quite sound, apart from the danger depicted by Dr. Bowley, as long as we had peace, or as long as the wars that happened were sufficiently restricted in their area and effect. But now we have seen that war may happen on such a scale as to make the interchange of products between nations a source of grave weakness to those who practise it, if it means that they are thereby in danger of finding themselves at war with the providers of things that they need for subsistence or for defence.

Another lesson that the war has taught us is that modern warfare enormously increases the cost of carriage by sea, because it shuts up in neutral harbours the merchant ships of the powers that are weaker on the sea, and makes huge calls, for transport purposes, on those of the powers which are in the ascendant on the water. This increase in the cost of sea carriage adds to the cost of all goods that come by sea, and is a particularly important item in the bill that we, as an island people, have to pay for the luxury of war. It is true that much of the high price of freight goes into the pockets of our shipowners, but they, being busy with transport work for the Government, cannot take nearly so much advantage of it as the shipmasters of neutral countries.

The economic argument, then, that it pays best to make and grow things where they can best be made and grown remains just as true as ever it was, but it has been complicated by a political objection that if one happens to go to war with a nation that has supplied raw material, or half-raw material, for industries that are essential to our commercial if not to our actual existence, the good profits made in time of peace are likely to be wiped out, or worse, by the extent of the inconvenience and paralysis that this dependence brings with it in time of war. And even if we are not at war with our providers, the greater danger and cost of carriage by sea, when war is afoot, makes us question the advantage of the process, for example, by which we have developed a foreign dairying industry with our capital, and learnt to depend on it for a large part of our supply of eggs and butter, while at home we have seen a great magnate lay waste farms in order to make fruitful land into a wilderness for himself and his deer. It may have paid us to let this be done if we were sure of peace, but now that we have seen what modern warfare means, when it breaks out on a big scale, we may surely begin to think that people who make bracken grow in place of wheat, in order to improve what auctioneers call the amenities of their rural residences, are putting their personal gratification first in a question which is of national importance.

We may seem to have strayed far from the problems of International Finance and the free interchange of capital between countries, but in fact we are in the very middle of them, because they are so complicated and diverse that they affect nearly every aspect of our national lives. By sending capital abroad we make other countries produce for us and so we help a tendency by which we grow less at home, and export coupons, or demands for interest, instead of the present produce of our brains and muscles; and we do much more than that, for we thereby encourage the best of our workers to leave our shores and seek their fortunes in the new lands which our capital opens up. When we export capital it goes in the shape of goods and services, and it is followed by an export of men, who go to lands where land is plentiful and cheap, and men are scarce and well paid. This process again was sound enough from the purely economic point of view. It quickened the growth of the world's wealth by putting men of enterprise in places where their work was most handsomely rewarded, and their lives were unhampered by the many bars to success that remnants of feudalism and social restrictions put in their way in old countries; and it cleared the home labour market and so helped the workers in their uphill struggle for better conditions and a chance of a real life. But when the guns begin to shoot, the question must arise whether we were wise in leaving the export of capital, which has such great and complicated effects, entirely to the influence of the higgling of the market, and the price offered by the highest bidder.

Much will evidently depend on the way in which the present war ends. If it should prove to be, as so many hoped at its beginning, a "war to end war," and should be followed by a peace so well and truly founded that we need have no fear for its destruction, then there will be much to be said for leaving economic forces to work themselves out by economic means, subject to any checks that their social effects may make necessary. But if, as seems to be probable, the war ends in a way that makes other such wars quite possible, when we have all recovered from the exhaustion and disgust produced by the present one, then political expediency may overrule economic advantage, and we may find it necessary to consider the policy of restricting the export of British capital to countries with which there is no chance of our ever being at war, and especially to our own Dominions oversea, not necessarily by prohibitions and hard and fast rules, but rather by seeing that the countries to which it is desirable for our capital to go may have some advantage when they appeal for it.

This advantage our own colonial Dominions already possess, both from the sentiment of investors, which is a strong influence in their favour, and will be stronger than ever after the war, and from legal enactment which allows trustees to invest trust funds in their loans. Probably the safest course would be to leave sentiment to settle the matter, and pray to Providence to give us sensible sentiments. Actual restraints on the export of capital would be very difficult to enforce, for capital is an elusive commodity that cannot be stopped at the Customs houses. If we lent money to a friendly nation, and our friend was thereby enabled to lend to a likely foe, we should not have mended matters. The time is not yet ripe for a full discussion of this difficult and complicated question, and it is above all important that we should not jump to hasty conclusions about it while under the influence of the feverish state of mind produced by war. The war has shown us that our wealth was a sure and trusty weapon, and much of the strength of this weapon we owe to our activity in International Finance.

FOOTNOTES:

[7]

"England's Foreign Trade in the Nineteenth Century," p, 16, by Dr. A.L. Bowley.

[8]

"Paper against Gold," Letter III.

CHAPTER VIII

REMEDIES AND REGULATIONS

Apart from the political measures which may be found necessary for the regulation, after the war, of International Finance, it remains to consider what can be done to amend the evils from which it suffers, and likewise what, if anything, can be done to strengthen our financial weapon, and sharpen its edge to help us in the difficult fight that will follow the present war, however it may end.

It has been shown in a previous chapter that the real weaknesses in the system of International Finance arise from the bad use made of its facilities by improvident and corrupt borrowers, and from the bigger profits attached, in the case of success, to the more questionable kinds of issues. With regard to the latter point it was also shown that these bigger profits may be, to a great extent, justified by the fact that the risk involved is much greater; since in the case of failure a weak security is much more difficult to finance and find a home for than a good one. It may further be asked why weak securities should be brought out at all and whether it is not the business of financial experts to see that nothing but the most water-tight issues are offered to the public. Such a question evidently answers itself, for if only those borrowers were allowed to come into the market whose credit was beyond doubt, the growth of young communities and of budding enterprises would be strangled and the forward movement of material progress would be seriously checked.

It is sometimes contended that much more might be done by the Stock Exchange Committee in taking measures to see that the securities to which it grants quotations and settlements are soundly based. If this view is to prevail, its victory has been greatly helped by the events of the war, during which the Stock Exchange has seen itself regulated and controlled by outside authority to such an extent that it would be much readier than it was two years ago to submit to regulations imposed on it by its own Committee at the bidding of the Government. Nevertheless, there is this great difficulty, that as soon as the Stock Exchange begins to impose other than merely formal rules upon the issue of securities under its authority, the public very naturally comes to the conclusion that all securities brought out under its sanction may be relied on as absolutely secure; and since it is wholly impossible that the Committee's regulations could be so strict as to ensure this result without imposing limits that would have the effect of smothering enterprise, the effect of any such attempt would be to encourage the public to pursue a happy-go-lucky system of investing, and then to blame the Stock Exchange if ever it found that it had made a mistake and had indulged in speculation when it flattered itself that it was investing. The whole question bristles with difficulties, but it seems hardly likely that after the war the Stock Exchange and the business of dealing in securities will ever be quite on the old basis again.

In any attempt that is made to regulate them, however, it will be very necessary to remember that capital is an extremely elusive thing, and that if too strict rules are laid down for it, it very easily evades them by transferring itself to other centres. If the authorities decide that only such and such issues are to be made, or such and such securities are to be dealt in in London, they will be inviting those who consider such regulations unfair or unwise to buy a draft on Paris or New York, and invest their money in a foreign centre. Capital is easily scared, and is very difficult to bottle up and control, and if any guidance of it in a certain direction is needed, the object would probably be much more easily achieved by suggestion than by any attempt at hard and fast restriction, such as worked well enough under the stress of war.

Any real improvement to be achieved in the system by which we have hitherto supplied other nations with capital will ultimately have to be brought about by a keener appreciation, both by issuing houses and investors, of the kind of business that is truly legitimate and profitable. It does not pay in the long run to supply young communities with opportunities for outrunning the constable, and it is possible that when this wholesome platitude is more clearly grasped by the public, no issuing house will be found to bring out a loan that is not going to be used for some definite reproductive purpose, or to float a company, even of the semi-speculative kind, the prospects of which have not been so well tested that the shareholders are at least bound to have a fair chance of success. The ideals of the issuing houses have so far advanced since the days of the Honduras scandal, that in the time of the late war in the Balkans none could be found to father any financial operation in London on behalf of any of the warring peoples. It only remains for the education of the investor to continue the progress that it has lately made, for the waste of capital by bad investment to be greatly curtailed. Probably there will always, as long as the present financial basis of society lasts, be outbursts of speculation in which a greedy public will rush madly after certain classes of stocks and shares, with the result that a few cool-headed or lucky gamblers will be able to live happily ever after as country gentlemen, and transmit comfortable fortunes to their descendants for all time. This is the debt that society pays for its occasional lapses in finance, just as its lapses in matters of taste are paid for by the enriching of those who provide it with rubbishy stuff to read, or rubbishy shows in picture palaces. The education of the individual in the matter of spending or investing his or her money is one of the most pressing needs of the future, and only by its progress can the evils which are usually laid to the door of finance be cured by being attacked in their real home. In the meantime much might be done by more candid publicity and clearer statements in prospectuses of the objects for which money lent is to be used and of the terms on which loan issues have been arranged. Any reasonable attempts that may be made to improve the working of International Finance are certain to have the support of the best elements in the City.

At the same time we may hope that as economic progress goes slowly ahead over the stepping stones of uncomfortable experience, borrowing countries will see that it really pays them to pay their yearly bills out of yearly taxes, and that they are only hurting themselves when they mortgage their future revenue for loans, the spending of which is not going to help them to produce more goods and so raise more revenue without effort. War is the only possible excuse for asking foreign nations to find money for other than reproductive purposes. In time of war it can be justified, even as an individual can be justified for drawing on his capital in order to pay for an operation that will save his life. But in both cases it leaves both the nation and the individual permanently poorer and with a continuous burden to meet in the shape of interest and sinking fund, until the loan has been redeemed. Loans raised at home have an essentially different effect. The interest on them is raised from the taxpayers and paid back to the taxpayers, and the nation, as a whole, is none the poorer. But when one nation borrows from another it takes the loan in the form of goods or services, and unless these goods and services are used in such a way as to enrich it and help it to produce goods and services itself, it is bound to be a loser by the bargain; because it has to pay interest on the loan in goods and services and to redeem the loan by the same process, and if the loan has not been used to increase its power of turning out goods and services, it is inevitably in the same position as a spendthrift individual who has pledged his income for an advance and spent it on riotous living.

One of the great benefits that the present war is working is that it is teaching young countries to do without continual drafts of fresh capital from the older ones. Instead of being able to finance themselves by fresh borrowing, they have had to close their capital accounts for the time being, and develop themselves out of their own resources. It is a very useful experience for them, and is teaching them lessons that will stand them in good stead for some time to come. For the old countries, when the war is over, will have problems of their own to face at home, and will not be able at once to go back to the old system of placing money abroad, even if they should decide that the experiences of war have raised no objections to their doing so with the old indiscriminate freedom.

It is easy, however, to exaggerate the effect of the war on our power to finance other peoples. Pessimistic observers, with a pacifist turn of mind, who regard all war as a hideous barbarism and refuse to see that anything good can come out of it, are apt in these days to make our flesh creep by telling us that war will inevitably leave Europe so exhausted and impoverished that its financial future is a prospect of unmitigated gloom. They talk of the whole cost of the war as so much destruction of capital, and maintain that by this destruction we shall be for some generations in a state of comparative destitution. These gloomy forecasts may be right, but I hope and believe that they will be found to have been nightmares, evolved by depressed and prejudiced imaginations. War destroys capital when and where actual destruction of property takes place, as now in Belgium, Northern France, and other scenes of actual warfare, and on the sea, where a large number of ships, though small in relation to the total tale of the merchant navies of the world, have been sunk and destroyed. Destruction in this sense has only been wrought, so far, in limited areas. In so far as agricultural land has been wasted, kindly nature, aided by industry and science, will soon restore its productive power. In so far as factories, railways, houses and ships have been shattered, man's power to make, increased to a marvellous extent by modern mechanical skill, will repair the damage with an ease and rapidity such as no previous age has witnessed.

In another sense it may be argued that war destroys capital in that it prevents its being accumulated, but this is a distortion of the meaning of the word destroy. If it had not been for the war, we in England should have been saving our usual three to four hundred millions a year and putting the money to productive uses, in so far as we did not lend it to spendthrift nations or throw it away on unprofitable ventures. If we had invested it well, it would have made us and the rest of the world richer. Instead of doing so we are spending our savings on war and consequently we are not growing richer. But when the war is over our material productive power will be as great as ever, except for the small number of our ships that have been sunk or the small amount of damage done to us by enemy aircraft. Our railways and factories may be somewhat behindhand in upkeep, but that will soon be made good, and against that item on the debit side, we may set the great new organization for munition works, part of which, we may hope, will be available for peaceful production when the time for peace is ripe.

It is a complete mistake to suppose that war can be carried on out of accumulated capital, which is thereby destroyed. All the things and services needed for war have to be produced as the war goes on. The warring nations start with a stock of ships and guns and military and naval stores, but the wastage of them can only be made good by the production of new stuff and new clothes and food for the soldiers and new services rendered as the war goes on. This new production may be done either by the warring powers or by neutrals, and if it is done by neutrals, the warring powers can pay for it out of capital by selling their securities or by pledging their wealth. In so far as this is done the warring powers impoverish themselves and the neutrals are enriched, but the world's capital as a whole is not impaired. If we sell our Pennsylvania Railroad bonds to Americans, and buy shells with the proceeds, we are thereby poorer and Americans are richer, but the earning power of the Pennsylvania Railroad is not altered. It may be, if we conduct the war wastefully, and refuse to meet its cost by our own self-denial—going without things ourselves so that we can save, money to lend to the Government for the war—that we shall pledge our property and sell what of it we can sell to neutrals, to such an extent that we shall be seriously poorer at the end of it. At present[2] we are not selling and pledging our capital wealth any faster than we are lending to our Allies; and if we pull ourselves up short, and exercise the necessary self-denial, seeing that we must pay for the war in the long run out of our own pockets, and that far the cheapest and cleanest policy is to do so now, and if the war does not last too long, there is no reason why it should impoverish us to an extent that will cripple us seriously.

It is true that we shall have lost an appalling number of the best of our manhood, and this is a loss that is irreparable in many of its aspects. But from the purely material point of view we may set against it the great increase in the productive power of those that are left behind, through the lessons that the war has taught us in using the store of available energy that was idle among us before. We shall have learnt to work as we never worked before, and we shall have learnt that many of the things on which we used to waste our money and energy were unworthy of us at all times and especially at a time of national crisis. If we can only recognize that the national crisis will go on after the war, and will go on until we have made this old country civilized in the real sense of the word, that is, free from destitution and the vice and dirt and degradation and disease that go with it, then our power of recovery after the war will be illimitable, and we shall go forward to a new standard of wealth and national duty that will leave the dingy ideals of the nineteenth century behind us like a bad dream. This may seem somewhat irrelevant to the question of International Finance, but it is not so. We led the way in spreading our capital over the world, with little or no regard for the consequences of this policy on the condition of our population at home. We have now, in the great regeneration that this war has brought, and will bring in still greater measure, to show that we can still make and save capital faster than ever, by working harder and spending our money on improving our heritage, instead of on frivolity and self-indulgence. Then we shall still be free to lend money to borrowers who will use it well, and at the same time have plenty to spare for wise use at home in clearing the blots off our civilization.

FOOTNOTES:

[9]

Written on New Year's Eve, 1915.

CPSIA information can be obtained
at www.ICGtesting.com
Printed in the USA
LVHW090448081122
732583LV00005B/230